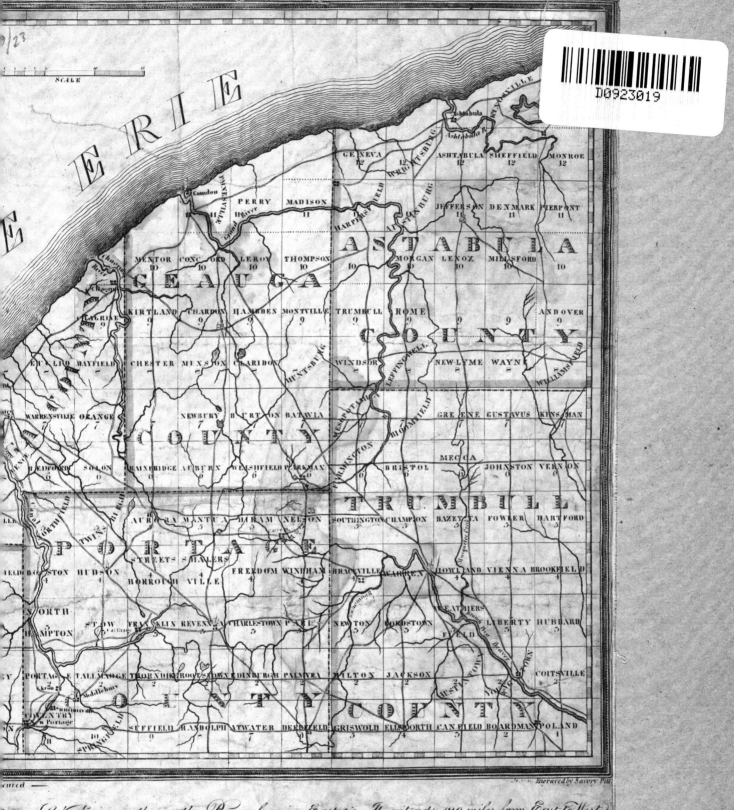

SCALE

E R I E

E

ERIE

GENEVA 12 · WRIGHTSBURG 12 · ASHTABULA 12 · SHEFFIELD 12 · MONROE 12

Grandon · PAINESVILLE · PERRY 11 · MADISON 11 · HARPERSFIELD · AUSTINBURG · JEFFERSON 11 · DENMARK 11 · PIERPONT 11

Grand River

MENTOR 10 · CONCORD 10 · LEROY 10 · THOMPSON 10 · 10 · MORGAN 10 · LENOX 10 · MILLSFORD 10 · 10

GEAUGA

Chagrin Rev

LAGRANGE 9 · KIRTLAND 9 · CHARDON 9 · HAMBDEN 9 · MONTVILLE 9 · TRUMBULL 9 · ROME 9 · 9 · ANDOVER 9

C O U N T Y

EUCLID · MAYFIELD · CHESTER · MUNSON · CLARIDON · HUNTSBURG · WINDSOR · LEFFINGWELL · NEW-LYME · WAYNE · WILLIAMSFIELD

WARRENSVILLE 7 · ORANGE 7 · NEWBURY · BURTON · BATAVIA · MESOPOTAMIA · BLOOMFIELD · GREENE 7 · GUSTAVUS 7 · KINSMAN 7

C O U N T Y

BEDFORD · SOLON · BAINBRIDGE · AUBURN · WELSHFIELD · PARKMAN 6 · FARMINGTON · BRISTOL 6 · MECCA 6 · JOHNSTON 6 · VERNON 6

NORTHFIELD · TWINSBURG · AURORA · MANTUA 5 · HIRAM 5 · NELSON 5 · SOUTHINGTON 5 · CHAMPION 5 · BAZETTA 5 · FOWLER 5 · HARTFORD 5

P O R T A G E

T R U M B U L L

BOSTON · HUDSON 4 · STREETSBORO · MALERS 4 · FREEDOM 4 · WINDHAM 4 · BRACEVILLE · WARREN 4 · HOWLAND 4 · VIENNA 4 · BROOKFIELD 4

BORROUGH VILLE

NORTHAMPTON · STOW 3 · FRANKLIN · RAVENNA 3 · CHARLESTOWN · PARIS 3 · NEWTON 3 · JORDSTOWN · WEATHERSFIELD · LIBERTY 3 · HUBBARD 3

Carthage · FIELD

PORTAGE 2 · TALLMADGE · THORNDIKE · ROOTSTOWN · EDINBURGH · PALMYRA 2 · MILTON 2 · JACKSON 2 · AUSTINTOWN · COITSVILLE 2

Akron 2 · Middlebury · Saddlebury

COVENTRY · New Portage

SPRINGFIELD · SUFFIELD · RANDOLPH 9 · ATWATER · DEERFIELD · GRISWOLD · ELLSWORTH 4 · CANFIELD 2 · BOARDMAN 2 · POLAND

C O U N T Y   C O U N T Y

Engraved by Savery Phil.

...ween Lake Erie on the north, Pennsylvania East &c. It extends 120 miles from East to West)
...body of 500,000 of acres is stricken off from the west end of the tract, and granted by the state of
...h during the Revolutionary War, the manner by which the state of Connecticut became possessed
...the example of his brother kings, of granting distant and foreign regions to his subjects granted
...in certain specified bounds. But as the geographical knowledge of Europeans concerning America
...er. — After the United States became an Independent Nation, these interfering claims occasioned
...s finally compromised by the United States relinquishing their claim to the 3,000,000 of acres described
...en united this tract to the Territory now State of Ohio.

A Pictorial History of the Western Reserve
1796 to 1860

Margaret M. Butler

Jan 16, 1971

To Bert Dunphy
with best wishes

Bill Holden

Recollections by S. G. Goodrich

A

Pictorial History

Of The Western Reserve

1796 to 1860

By Margaret Manor Butler

A JOINT PUBLICATION

The Early Settlers Association of the Western Reserve

The Western Reserve Historical Society

The World Publishing Company

CLEVELAND, OHIO

Published by The World Publishing Company
2231 West 110th Street, Cleveland, Ohio 44102
All rights reserved. Printed in the U.S.A.
1GLWP1065

Publication of this book has been made possible
by the General Fund of
The Early Settlers Association of the Western Reserve
Publication Number 1-63

and by the Clara Belle Ritchie Trust Fund of
The Western Reserve Historical Society
W.R.H.S. Publication Number 117

FRONTISPIECE

Emigration from Connecticut in the early 1800's was far from pleasurable. Poor roads posed one of the greatest problems. Entire families found themselves walking most of the way to lighten the load because the uphill muddy roads were too difficult for the horses or oxen to scale. Corduroy roads looked welcome at a distance, but many preferred walking to the jarring, nerve-shattering bumps of the wooden wheels on irregular logs. Often horses collapsed from fatigue and wagons were abandoned by the roadside for lack of repair parts.

Foreword

The Early Settlers Association of the Western Reserve and The Western Reserve Historical Society, both organizations dedicated to the preservation of the culture and tradition of the Western Reserve, are joint sponsors of this book.

We have long felt the need for a pictorial history of the Western Reserve and because of increasing requests for an accurate and attractive work of this kind, we chose Margaret Manor Butler, well-known author, scholar, and official historian of the Early Settlers Association, to write and produce such a narrative. Preparation of text and selection of pictures by Mrs. Butler occupied almost two years, crowded with hours of research, study, correspondence, and trips through the area. She has chosen only the finest pictures and to accompany each has written a concise historical account.

We believe her scholarship, her high standards, her exhaustive research have produced a valuable work to which future students of history may refer with confidence and to which the average reader may turn with enjoyment.

THE EARLY SETTLERS ASSOCIATION OF THE WESTERN RESERVE

Donald L. Harbaugh, *President*

THE WESTERN RESERVE HISTORICAL SOCIETY

Herman L. Vail, *President*

September 10, 1963

To

Contemporary and future historians
who might find in this pictorial record
of the early nineteenth-century Western Reserve
source material on which to base further original research.

And To

Commodore Oliver Hazard Perry
who one hundred fifty years ago at Put-in-Bay
helped protect and insure
the continuance of Western Reserve culture.

September 10, 1963

Contents

Introduction

After the Revolutionary War and the formation of the United States all the colonies made special concessions of their western lands to the federal government. Connecticut was the only state allowed to reserve a section. It was situated in the northern part of Ohio along Lake Erie, a strip 120 miles long extending from the Pennsylvania border to a little west of Sandusky, and approximately 75 miles wide reaching from Lake Erie to a few miles below Youngstown. To this day the section is referred to as the Western Reserve of Connecticut, calling attention to the unique role Connecticut played in the development of the early settlements.

For a number of years this area was a colony of the mother state and remained outside the jurisdiction of the federal government's vast Northwest Territory. Part of the Western Reserve, called the Firelands, was given to Connecticut citizens who had suffered losses during the Revolution; one tract, rich in salt, was sold to a single individual; but the largest area, three million acres, was purchased by the privately controlled Connecticut Land Company for about forty cents an acre. The company in turn surveyed the land and sold acreage and entire townships to New England purchasers. Many rural areas still retain the eighteenth-century Connecticut characteristics in their dwellings, churches, town squares, and village names.

As the agent for the Connecticut Land Company, Moses Cleaveland led the first surveying party in 1796 with explicit orders to lay out a town at the mouth of the Cuyahoga and to subdivide the Western Reserve into townships. This Pictorial History of the Western Reserve illustrates the kind of terrain which greeted him and his surveyors. It depicts the type of homes the early pioneers built, how their educational system grew, how religion, politics, recreation, and the arts influenced their lives and how their industry developed. Sketches, woodcuts, paintings, and photographs have been chosen with great care to tell, as accurately as possible, this story of the period from the arrival of Moses Cleaveland to the year 1860.

MARGARET MANOR BUTLER

PART ONE

Conquering the Wilderness

Members of Moses Cleaveland's surveying party had not the faintest idea of the hardships they would endure after their arrival in the Western Reserve. Frustrations, weariness, and discouragement faced them each grueling day of the survey. They suffered from inadequate shelter, over-exertion, and a miserable diet. Nearly everyone contracted the ague (malaria) or dysentery. Although nearly all members of the party had received grants of land, they were not tempted to stay in the Reserve. They were glad to return to civilization and very few ever came back.

But most of the pioneers who loaded their covered wagons with all their possessions and traveled to the Reserve were unable to return East no matter how disappointed or disillusioned they became. Either they had no home to which to return, or no funds to make the trip. Furthermore, they would have been humiliated by admitting that they had not found a land of milk and honey. Some, of course, expected only bitter struggle against the wilderness, and willingly labored to achieve success.

For almost thirty years settlers in isolated areas struggled to eke out a living, raising their own food, building their own cabins, making necessary furniture, utensils, and clothing. In settling the wilderness they had no precedent to follow except that left by the Indians who had occupied the Reserve prior to their coming. They used the Indian trails to lay out their crude roads which often led to salt licks, springs, and clearings of former village sites. Not until the 1820's did the rigors of frontier living begin to give way to an easier, more comfortable way of life.

Surveying the Western Reserve

LEFT ABOVE

Moses Cleaveland (1750–1825), a graduate of Yale and a lawyer, made a land purchase of $32,600 and was selected as the agent of the Connecticut Land Company. In company with civil engineers, mathematicians, surveyors, an astronomer, a commissary, boatmen, and many helpers, he undertook the long trip to the Western Reserve in May, 1796. His instructions were to make treaties with the Indians, to lay out a city, and to lead the survey of the entire Western Reserve.

RIGHT ABOVE

To Seth Pease (1764–1819) we are indebted for a good share of the Western Reserve Survey. He came with Moses Cleaveland in 1796 as astronomer and surveyor, and returned the following year as chief surveyor. In 1806 he was commissioned by the United States government to survey the area west of the Cuyahoga River. He made a map of Cleveland at the time of the first survey and one of the Western Reserve two years later. His field books and journals have been valuable sources of information. During the Jefferson and Madison administrations he served as assistant postmaster to General Gideon Granger, his brother-in-law.

RIGHT

This early map of the Connecticut Western Reserve was made from the actual survey by Seth Pease and Abraham Tappen in 1798. Also shown is the type of chain used in surveying. Below is the original book of Surveys of Townships. One example is the 47th draft made by Daniel L. Coit and others.

LEFT

This silhouette of James Kingsbury (1767–1847) is probably the only likeness of him ever made. As the first permanent settler in the Western Reserve, he is symbolic of the hardy pioneers who struggled against great odds to carve out homesteads and establish law-abiding communities in the wilderness. In June, 1796, with his wife and three children under three, a thirteen-year-old nephew, a horse, a cow, and a yoke of oxen, he left a comfortable home in Alsted, New Hampshire, to seek his fortune in the west. They arrived at Conneaut shortly after Moses Cleaveland's surveying party, hence their earliest stay was not so desolate. After the surveyors left, James found it necessary to go back to New Hampshire, leaving his family alone. He expected to return in about a month, but fever and misfortune overtook him. It was two months before he crossed his threshold again only to find his new-born son dying of malnutrition and his wife at death's door. Their trials are a heart-breaking story. They followed the second surveying party to Cleveland, and eventually settled in Newburgh. In 1800 James Kingsbury was appointed Judge of the Court of Common Pleas for Trumbull County. Later he became Justice of the Peace and collector of taxes. In 1805 he was elected a member of the Ohio Legislature.

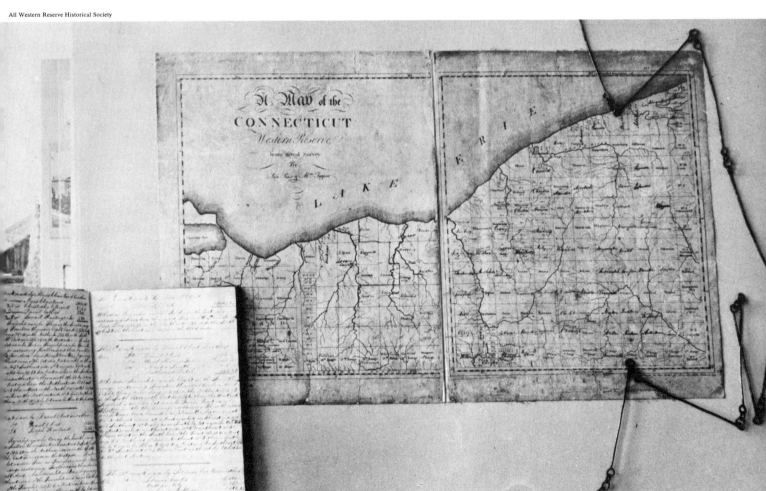

Settlers' Dream

Ohio State Historical Society

City of Cuyahoga Falls

LEFT ABOVE

This advertisement from the *American Mercury* (Hartford, Connecticut) for September 13, 1804, is typical of many telling about the lush farmlands for sale in New Connecticut, Trumbull County.

ABOVE

The lure of cheap land, fertile fields, and wild game aplenty drew New England farmers, discouraged with their own unproductive soil, to the Western Reserve so often pictured as the land of milk and honey. Visions of sturdy cabins, warm and snug against the wintry blasts, with stalwart men and boys bringing home the bounty secured after a day of hunting, filled the thoughts of many an emigrant.

LEFT

Stories of powerful falls, the natural sites for necessary mills, were an added inducement to settle in the Western Reserve. The Big Falls of the Cuyahoga in the vicinity of Old Maid's Kitchen was the site of a large village of the Delawares under Chief Net-a-wat-wees.

RIGHT

This copy of a painting of James A. Garfield's birthplace in Orange authentically illustrates his early life in a log cabin, surrounded by the actual children with whom he played. Young Garfield is carrying the rock across the pond. The log cabin on the hill was his schoolhouse.

FAR RIGHT

Edwin Tunis has vividly captured the utter dejection of the early pioneers as they wade through mud behind their covered wagon instead of riding in it. The corduroy road consisted of logs laid across swampy areas.

Stark Reality

ABOVE

Too often the vision of a land of plenty faded against the stark reality of an amateur trying to build a home with few tools and lack of experience or of a housewife unaccustomed to the rigors and privations of pioneer living, struggling to clothe and cook for a family.

RIGHT ABOVE

Lorenzo Carter (1766-1814), Cleveland's first permanent settler, brought his family from Rutland, Vermont, on May 2, 1797, to a hastily constructed log cabin at the mouth of the Cuyahoga River. He was the most fearless and versatile of the early pioneers, noted for his brusque exterior but kind heart underneath. When malaria drove others away from the stagnant river, he stubbornly stayed on, constructed a ferry and continued to plant several acres of corn on Water Street. An excellent marksman, enthusiastic hunter, and wily trader with the Indians, he kept his family well fed and clothed. As the first constable in the township and captain in the Ohio Militia, he was the law for Indians and whites. His tavern served needs for the surrounding area. Here the first school was started, mail and news from the East dispensed, and the first ball was held. In 1808 he launched the thirty-ton Zephyr, first boat suitable for lake trading.

5

Tramping Indian Trails

LEFT ABOVE
When Doan Brook was a meandering stream in Wade Park, Cleveland, it looked like this.

ABOVE
One way the early Indian tribes had of communicating with each other was by marking trees. There is a logical theory that this giant white oak was deformed about 200 years ago to indicate the trail between the north terminal of Portage Path and the waters of the Cuyahoga River above the gorge. It is located on the Goudy farm, Cuyahoga Falls, between Peck Road and the river.

LEFT
Old Maid's Kitchen, Cuyahoga Falls, an historic rock cave on the north bank of the Cuyahoga River, once overlooked a large Indian village. Many stories have been handed down of raids and massacres and of white women and children captured and hidden here. It is now part of the Metropolitan Park and open to the public.

OPPOSITE: TOP
The mouth of Rocky River has changed very little since its earliest days.

6

ABOVE

For unknown centuries, Portage Path was used by the Indians to carry, or port, their canoes between the Cuyahoga River and the Tuscarawas River, a distance of slightly more than eight miles in the present city of Akron. Except for this portage, it was possible for the Indians to travel from the Great Lakes to the Gulf of Mexico by water. In 1785 by a treaty with the Indians, Portage Path was made the western dividing line between the United States and Indian territory. The full length of the trail has been marked by metal signs.

RIGHT ABOVE

As the Huron River, north of Monroeville, looked to the Indians and the early settlers.

RIGHT

Peaceful calm pervades the banks of the Black River, near Elyria.

7

This primitive portrait group of the Ruggles family of Vermilion was made by an unknown nineteenth-century itinerant artist who visited their home and captured their likenesses on the spot. The artist applied his paint in a flat and simple manner with little knowledge of foreshortening.

PART TWO

The Simple Life

After the initial struggle of clearing the land and building primitive dwellings, the Reserve settlers strove to achieve a more integrated and regulated community life than had been possible in the earlier years. They had learned to make a good living from the land and had developed small handcraft enterprises. With moderate prosperity came the establishment of towns which exchanged the handwork of local artisans for farm products and served as centers for limited trade with the East. The interest of the settlers turned from individual struggle for existence toward problems of community organization and the gaining of local social prestige. Life was no longer a struggle for survival, and not yet a hectic rush toward industrialization.

In their new ease and self-sufficiency, the settlers sought to duplicate certain aspects of the culture they had left behind in New England. They replaced their crude log structures with homes, churches and schools of frame and clapboard patterned after buildings in the East. They often planned towns and organized local governments in the New England manner. They early established elementary schools, academies, and colleges similar to those they had known in their old home towns. Their simple, unhurried life was not to last long, however. The canals and railroads brought new goods, new competition, new industries to the Reserve, and increased the pace of living. Traditional culture was broadened by the influx of new ideas. Local quietude gave way to a busy commercial and industrial life.

9

Early Scenes

OPPOSITE: TOP TO BOTTOM

The simplicity of early Cleveland Village was captured in these sketches by Thomas Whelpley in 1833.

Pigs are wallowing in the mud next to the new three-story Cleveland City Hotel (the site of our present Cleveland-Sheraton Hotel). The low building opposite on Superior and the Square was Reuben Wood's law office, where he practiced before he became Governor. The church to the right is Trinity at St. Clair and Seneca. The lighthouse, on Water Street, can be seen in the center. Practically all the business of the village was conducted on Superior west of Public Square.

Looking east from the corner of Bank and St. Clair streets in Cleveland, one can see from left to right: the "Old Academy," Trinity Church, Old Stone Church, Courthouse (extreme right).

Cows grazed where East Sixth Street intersects Euclid Avenue today. The building in the center is the County Courthouse on the Square. The tall tower to the right is Old Stone Church.

From a pastoral scene on the west side of the Cuyahoga, one glimpses the growing village of Cleveland in 1833.

BELOW

This charming primitive by Sebastian Heine shows the southwest corner of Cleveland's Public Square as it might have looked to the artist in the late 1830's. The second courthouse (site of the present Higbee's) was an impressive building with Doric facade and Ionic columns supporting the cupola. The spire to the right belonged to the First Baptist Church, built in 1836 on Seneca at Champlain. At the right is Cleveland House, erected in 1832 on the site of the present Cleveland-Sheraton Hotel. The artist has made the square look beautiful and immaculate, unlike contemporary descriptions which had pigs and cattle roaming the area and few pedestrians dressed in the latest fashion.

ABOVE

The Cleveland Grays attracted admiring groups of citizens as they marched in the 1839 Fourth of July parade on the Public Square, prominently displaying their new silk flag. Old Stone Church, dedicated in 1834, dominated the north side of the Square. The building to the extreme left (where Marshall Drug now stands) was the store of George Hill, who also did carpenter and joiner jobs on occasion. There were offices above for the well-known attorneys and counselors, Silliman, Stetson and Barr. Judge John Barr, as secretary of the Pioneer Society, had collected valuable incidents and biographies of the early days, some of them incorporated in Whittlesey's *History of Cleveland*. The large house to the right of the church (now the site of Society National Bank) was the home of N. E. Crittenden, dealer in jewelry, hardware, and fancy goods. This painting has been attributed to Sebastian Heine or Heine and Lewis Chavalier.

BELOW

Henry Howe, who made this sketch of Akron in 1846, described it as the Summit County seat and as a large and flourishing town on the Ohio Canal at the junction of the Pennsylvania Canal. It had eight churches, twenty mercantile stores, ten groceries, four drug and two book stores, four woolen factories, two blast and three small furnaces, a carding machine factory, five flour mills, an insurance company, a bank, two newspapers, and a great variety of mechanical establishments. At the time of the opening of the canal in 1827, with a sizable influx of Irish laborers, the population was about 600. By 1840 it had reached 1,664, and at the end of six years it had doubled. Here was the promise of a great industrial town.

Made by John Kilburn of Cincinnati in 1856, this sketch shows the new fountain with the steeple of Old Stone Church in the background. Kilburn said that "Cleveland, 255 miles northeast of Cincinnati, is an important and flourishing city. Commercial advantages are great, the harbor excellent. The Ohio Canal, various railroads, science and art help to make it the most commercial town in the state next to Cincinnati." In 1853 streets were lighted with gas; the population was 41,196. In 1856 as water was being let into new mains, a state fair was in progress on Public Square. A featured attraction was the "capacious fountain" from which thousands of visitors sampled drinking water. Local papers declared it was the first fountain in the state.

Cleveland's second courthouse, built in 1828 by Harry Noble and George C. Hill, not only served as a court for thirty years, but became a central meeting house for many activities—political, religious, and literary. This sketch was made by John Kilburn of Cincinnati in 1856. By 1858 plans were under way for building a third courthouse on the opposite side of Public Square.

BELOW
Warren, the county seat of Trumbull, is on the Mahoning River and the Ohio and Pennsylvania Canal. According to Henry Howe, who sketched this scene in 1846, it was a well-built and very pleasant town with a public square and a handsome courthouse. In 1800 Ephraim Quinby plotted the town, reserving four acres for a square, and naming it for Moses Warren, surveyor with the Moses Cleaveland party.

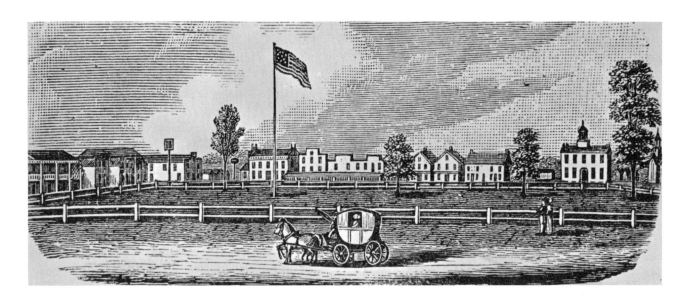

Medina's Public Square, sketched by Henry Howe in 1846, gives the impression of a neat and well laid-out town. To the far right are the old courthouse and the Baptist Church; at the extreme left is the American House. Prior to 1827 most of the settlers were engaged in agriculture to supply their own needs, but with the opening of the canal there was outside demand for their butter, cheese, and wheat. Later Medina became famous as a bee center, including not only the cultivation of bees but the manufacture of the implements needed.

OPPOSITE: MIDDLE

Youngstown in 1846 showed promise of a future industrial center. In this sketch by Henry Howe, smoke pours from a rolling mill of the Youngstown Iron Co., seen at the extreme left. In the distance a glimpse of the town shows the three spires of the Methodist, Disciples, and the Presbyterian churches. In the foreground are both the Mahoning River and the canal. Several coal mines were in successful operation, those of the Hon. David Tod producing about one hundred tons of coal a day. A large rolling mill was turning out bar, rod, and sheet iron. Small manufacturing establishments were producing tin-ware, cloth, axes, wagons, buggies, etc. As early as 1846 Youngstown, with a population of approximately 1,200, was one of the busiest towns in the Reserve.

OPPOSITE: BOTTOM

This is Poland's main street in the 1850's showing the unpaved road and rustic dwelling. The grist mill on the left was on Yellow Creek, dammed to furnish power.

BELOW

Chagrin Falls from the top of the hill west of town was sketched by Jehu Brainerd for Henry Howe in 1846. The falls, the bridge above it on Main Street, and the small industries near the dams of the river may be seen in the center. The building with the belfry (top right) is Asbury Seminary, built by Methodists and named for circuit-riding Bishop Asbury. It became the town's first public school in 1849 and has always been the site of a Chagrin Falls public school. Lower right is the Methodist Church, located across the street from the present church. The Congregational Church is at the left and the large building with two chimneys, just below the church, is the Bayard Tavern, popular stagecoach stop.

BELOW

Norwalk's West Main Street near Whittlesey Avenue shows the original Whittlesey Academy building at the corner. The low two-story frame was built as a tavern in 1825 by Obadiah Jenney. In 1830 he erected the four buildings to the left, only one of which remains, the one with the dormer next to the low building.

OPPOSITE: TOP

This photograph, taken about 1855, shows Norwalk's East Main Street at Linwood Ave., looking east. American House, built in 1836 by William Pitt Brown, is still standing as a storeroom and apartment building. The other large brick building to the left also survives. It may have been the house built by Lester Clark about 1824. The fence at the right surrounds the yard of Platt Benedict, founder of Norwalk, whose brick house, erected in 1819, is now incorporated in the Home Savings and Loan Company Building.

OPPOSITE: BOTTOM

Norwalk's Square at Main and Whittlesey shows a three-story brick, the original Whittlesey Academy, built in 1855 on land donated to the village by the founding fathers, Platt Benedict and Elisha Whittlesey. The low brick across the street was erected in 1830 as the county courthouse, and the two-story frame behind it is the original Huron County Jail, built by Platt Benedict in 1819.

LEFT

Platt Benedict, Norwalk's first permanent settler, brought his family from Danbury, Connecticut, in July, 1817, in a covered wagon drawn by one horse. He also brought a saddle horse and another covered wagon, drawn by four oxen, loaded with household goods and provisions. After seven weeks of hardship and wearisome travel, the Benedicts arrived only to find the cabin, which Platt had built on a previous trip, burned to the ground. Another was constructed in haste. It was replaced in two years by a brick house, a prominent landmark of the village. Platt became a valued member of the community as an organizer of the first Episcopal Church, instigator of a paper and grist mill, and president of the Firelands Historical Society. He lived to be almost 92 years of age.

BELOW

The main street of Norwalk was sketched in 1846 by Jehu Brainerd for Henry Howe. Howe was impressed with the good taste in the homes and buildings and the two miles of beautiful maple shade trees lining the thoroughfare. In the distance to the extreme left is the steeple of Norwalk Seminary. The three-story building is American House and the low building is the grocery store. Platt Benedict's home is in back of the shade trees. Next is the Bank of Norwalk, then the courthouse and jail, and at the extreme right the house built by Daniel Tilden in 1820.

Homes

The early homes depicted in this section were built in the northern part of Ohio before 1860. They are fine examples of what may be termed "Western Reserve" architecture, for they derive from a combination of frontier needs and a rich New England architectural heritage. A number of the early builders, having served their apprenticeships under architects in the East, were familiar with the historic styles and had become proficient in the use of special tools needed for detailed carpentry. A few, like Jonathan Goldsmith or Lemuel Porter and his son Simeon, became the best-known master craftsmen of those early days. They developed exceptionally beautiful interpretations of the Greek Revival style, several examples of which have survived in areas around Hudson, Tallmadge, and Painesville.

However, the majority of the early builders were ordinary farmer-carpenters who carefully studied carpenter's manuals written by Asher Benjamin and Minard Lafever. These were the carpenters usually hired to replace primitive log cabins with sturdily constructed dwellings. As a rule they chose materials close at hand, building brick houses where good clay was obtainable, stone houses where stone was easily procured, and frame houses in the vicinity of sawmills. Often they erected very simple houses with no extraneous decoration, but occasionally a farmer-carpenter who had a flair for whittling used his talent to carve pillars, frets, intricate moldings, and fan lights.

Apprehensive of being labeled "provincial" by their relatives and friends in the East, these determined pioneers bent every effort to construct the kind of homes to which they had been accustomed or which they had admired before coming West. They were eager to prove that they, too, valued culture and a gracious way of living. As prosperity came to more settlers, due mainly to the opening of the Ohio Canal and the Milan Canal, their desire for better housing attracted other master craftsmen to the Reserve, and the result was an increase of more elaborate homes in the midst of the home-made variety.

Both styles, the simple and the more ornate, may be termed "Western Reserve" architecture for they grew out of the needs of a rapidly developing western area influenced by an eastern heritage. Many should be preserved as examples of the transition from struggling pioneer life to a more leisurely cultured way of living.

Milan Public Museum

The Ebenezer Andrews house, 200 South Main Street, Milan, built in 1825, is an excellent example of Greek Revival, so popular in the Western Reserve in the 1820's. Andrews, a lawyer and shrewd business executive, opened Milan's first bank and helped to promote the Milan Canal. He also owned several warehouses and speculated in wheat and other products.

19

OPPOSITE: TOP

Shandy Hall, Unionville, Ashtabula County, was built in 1815 and probably is the oldest frame house in the Western Reserve preserved in its original condition. It was built by Colonel Robert Harper, the youngest son of Alexander Harper, founder of the first permanent settlement in Ashtabula County. Descendants of Robert continued to live in the house until 1938 when it was opened to the public as a museum; it is now maintained by the Western Reserve Historical Society. The house contains fifteen rooms and is completely furnished with authentic antiques and an accumulation of household articles used over a period of 120 years.

OPPOSITE: MIDDLE

Huge rough beams are much in evidence in Shandy Hall's basement kitchen. The fireplace with built-in oven is just as originally constructed in 1815. On display are utensils used over the years.

OPPOSITE: BOTTOM

The Hezekiah Davis house was erected in 1835. It was painted red except for the top boards. These were painted black to indicate that it was an Underground Railway Station. It is on the Mechanicsville Road, Hartsgrove Township, Ashtabula County.

BELOW

Sycamore Hall was built in 1815 by Eliphalet Austin, one of the first settlers in Austinburg, Ashtabula County. A large room off one of the porches was used as a hiding place for slaves.

Ashtabula County Historical Society

21

Ashtabula County Historical Society

Kelley Family History by Herman A. Kelley

Donald L. Harbaugh

ABOVE

This is one of Ashtabula's more pretentious homes, built in 1851 for Henry E. Parsons, first president of the Farmer's Bank of Ashtabula by Architect Corso Crane. It is now a funeral home.

TOP LEFT

Alfred Kelley, best known as Cleveland Village's first president and father of the Ohio Canal, took three years to build this classic home (1815–1818), probably the first brick house in Cleveland. It stood on the west side of Water Street overlooking Lake Erie and was intended for his parents. Specifications had been sent to him by his mother in 1814. However, she died before it was completed and it therefore became the home to which he brought his bride. Here five of their children were born and here the family spent ten of their happiest years. Descendants of the Kelleys and historians have disagreed on whether the house was built of stone or brick. A letter written by Daniel, the father, to one of his sons on September 27, 1814, should be considered authentic: "The brick house will not be built until next season, owing to failure of masons."

BOTTOM LEFT

Ashtabula was settled by Mathew Hubbard in 1804. His homestead, one of the earliest in Ashtabula, has been preserved and is now called "North End Club."

22

ABOVE
This house, built about 1845, stands on Route 534, two miles south of Windsor. It is the largest of five octagon houses in Ashtabula County and is of special interest because of its circular staircase which winds up to the cupola at the center of the structure.

RIGHT
The Hynton house on Canal Road, Cuyahoga County, a two-story brick built about 1809, is probably the oldest house still standing in the Cuyahoga Valley. It is of simpler construction but similar in design to the Jonathan Hale homestead and Middle College at Hudson. It has been assumed that Colonel Lemuel Porter influenced the building of all three. In its early days it was a favorite stagecoach stop on the Pittsburgh-Cleveland route.

23

Elroy Sanford

ABOVE

The Rowfant Club (3028 Prospect Avenue), Cleveland's oldest and most exclusive literary club, is quite appropriately housed in Cleveland's oldest brick residence. Built in 1826, it was the home and tavern of Noble Merwin at Superior and Vine. In 1838 it was moved and reconstructed by his son George B. Merwin. Its new location was on a high knoll facing Euclid Avenue with a wide expanse of lawn in front, luxurious shrubs, flowers, shade trees, circling driveways, and footpaths over the entire acreage reaching to the present Central Avenue. It was quite a showplace in its day, but progress took its toll, for the house itself was in the pathway of the proposed extension of Prospect Avenue beyond East 30th. Once again the house was moved, only this time about seventy feet farther back on the same property where it faced Prospect instead of Euclid. Here the lovers of books (only men) meet regularly.

LEFT

This small stone house, seemingly built into the side of a hill, was erected about 1822–24 by a stone mason who took great pride in his workmanship. The lintels are huge hand-cut slabs of stone and the entire structure is so sturdily built it will withstand many more generations of weather and wear. It was built over a spring, traces of which may still be seen in the basement. The house is located at the intersection of Canal and Stone Roads in the Cuyahoga Valley, Cuyahoga County.

24

ABOVE

Oldest Stone House, Lakewood, Cuyahoga County. During the 1830's and 1840's most of the log cabins on the Detroit Road in Lakewood were replaced with stone houses similar to this one built in 1838 by John Honam, a Scottish weaver, who undoubtedly followed directions in Asher Benjamin's *Practical Carpenter* or *American Builder's Companion*. The house was moved to Lakewood Park in 1952 where it was authentically restored as a pioneer home, open free to the public, and maintained by the Lakewood Historical Society. In December, 1961, the Society and its curator were honored with the second annual award of the American Institute of Architects, Cleveland Branch, for "preserving for the community a dwelling that displays both charm and dignity and is an excellent architectural example of a Western Reserve pioneer home."

RIGHT ABOVE

This is a typical pioneer home fireplace scene as depicted in the restored Oldest Stone House in Lakewood.

RIGHT BELOW

Dr. Jared Potter Kirtland, Western Reserve's most outstanding naturalist, spent his forty most productive years (1837–1877) in this small stone house on Detroit Road in Lakewood, Cuyahoga County. His huge farm became an experimental laboratory in the production of unusual and improved fruits, exotic plants, rare shrubs, and trees. Visitors came from all parts of the world to see his beautiful garden.

25

Lakewood Historical Society

LEFT TOP

James Nicholson, the first permanent settler on Detroit Road in Lakewood, built this fine example of New England architecture in 1835. It is the oldest frame house in the city and is still standing opposite Nicholson Avenue on Detroit.

LEFT BOTTOM

The Reuben Osborn house, 29202 Lake Road, Bay Village, Cuyahoga County, was erected in 1814, probably the oldest house still standing west of the Cuyahoga River. Tradition says the lumber was sawed east of Cleveland and rafted on the lake to this site. The central chimney of soft wire-cut brick was burned in this area. The lime in the mortar was made from shells gathered along the lake shore. Some of the land purchased by Deacon Reuben Osborn from the Connecticut Land Company in 1811 is still in possession of his descendants.

BELOW

Moses Warren house, 3535 Ingleside Road, Shaker Heights, Cuyahoga County, was one of the first frame houses in the township. It was built in 1817 by Moses Warren, a Revolutionary War veteran, who together with his son Daniel founded Warrensville. It is one of the few remaining houses of that early period in the Cleveland area, still attractive and in good condition. The large foundation stones, cut from a quarry nearby, and the hand-hewn beams may be seen in the basement.

Bay Village Archives

Jerry Horton, *Cleveland Press*

Bay Village Archives

Milan Public Museum

RIGHT

Cahoon house, Bay Village, Cuyahoga County, now called the Rose Hill Museum, was erected by Joseph Cahoon, who came to this site in 1810. The timbers were hewn by hand. Since nails could only be secured in Pittsburgh, the building was pegged with tree nails. It is ironic that Cahoon invented the first nail-making machine in the United States and was defrauded of his patent by a dishonest clerk in that office who favored another but later applicant. The roof shows the Gothic influence and the porch the Greek Revival.

BELOW

Dr. Lehman Galpin, who attended Mrs. Edison when Thomas, her seventh child, was born, built this house in 1846. It is now the Milan Historical Museum, a veritable storehouse of antiques and early records of Milan and Erie County.

Edison's birthplace in Milan was built in 1842 by his father Samuel on the side of a hill, making three levels necessary. The floors are made of locust wood, which gives them unusual color. The old Milan Canal is still visible from the garden. The house is now a Museum, maintained by the Edison Birthplace Association. It contains many of the Edison family treasures.

Thomas Edison, at age ten in 1857, posed for this picture with his sister Harriet Anne. Although his formal education lasted only three months, he has been credited with more than a thousand inventions, of which the best known are the phonograph and incandescent electric light.

One of the Reserve's most dignified classic structures, with ornamented pediment supported by Ionic columns, is the Mitchell-Turner or Zenas King house in Milan at Center and Judson Streets. It was built in 1847–48 and not in 1828 as has been reported, according to Milan's historian, Wallace B. White, who has delved into the tax records. At one time it was the home of Zenas King, one of the first builders of iron bridges in the country.

Nathan Jenkins, a successful merchant, engaged in buying and selling wheat and other commodities, was also a part-time contractor. He built a warehouse, had a share in building the Milan Canal, and built this home at 37 Front Street, Milan, in 1836. It is one of the fine Greek Revival homes in the Reserve.

Milan Public Museum

Elroy Sanford

Elroy Sanford

ABOVE

This house, built by George Boughton in 1834, was moved from Ford Lane and North Cheshire to the Geauga County Pioneer Village, Burton. The doorway originally graced the Mastick Moffett house. It shows unusual detail in the carved frieze and oval medallions.

BELOW

This is one of the first three frame buildings erected in Milan in 1817. Originally built by David Hinman, it is located between Merry and Church Streets. It is a typical salt box house.

Milan Public Museum

The Law house, built in 1817 by Merritt Nettleton, an expert craftsman, is another fine example of New England architecture. It originally stood on the southwest corner of Burton Park but has been moved to Pioneer Village, established by the Geauga County Historical Society.

The frame section to the left of the Geauga County Historical Society, Burton, was built in 1799 for Thomas Umberfield and his family, who had been on the way to the Western Reserve for about two and a half months and had not slept in a house since they left Geneseo, New York, according to the diary of Turhand Kirtland in which he said that he helped to build the house and named it Umbervilles (Umberfields) Coffee House. The Museum proper was built in 1838 by Eleazer Hickox who married Stella, daughter of Thomas Umberfield. The Museum now houses the treasures of the Geauga County Historical Society.

Elroy Sanford

Elroy Sanford

Sandusky Register, "Stately Old Homes" series

LEFT

The Follett house, 404 Wayne Street, Sandusky, Erie County, was built in 1835–37 by Oran Follett and is considered an important example of Greek Revival. The divided, winding staircase and the basement doorway beneath the main entrance are unique for this area. The stone was quarried nearby. Oran Follett was editor and part owner of the *Ohio State Journal.* Early in the history of Sandusky he was associated with bank, railroad, and real estate interests. He helped in the founding of the Republican Party and was a staunch abolitionist.

LEFT BELOW

The Sturgis-Kennan-Fulstow house, Norwalk, Huron County, was built about 1834 for Thaddeus Sturgis. It was sold to Jairus Kennan and later to Phillip Fulstow. It has a Classic Revival front with a pediment supported by four octagonal columns. On the pediment is a huge oval sunburst. It was either designed and built by William Gale Meade or was remodeled by him.

RIGHT BELOW

The Vredenburgh-Gardiner home, with Doric columns and unusual gable, was built in Norwalk by John Vredenburgh of old New York Dutch stock in the early 1830's. It was purchased in the 1850's by John Gardiner and has been occupied by members of that family ever since. The grounds have been beautifully landscaped.

Margaret M. Butler

Margaret M. Butler

The Firelands Historical Museum, Norwalk, Huron County, was known for many years as the Preston-Wickham house. It was built in 1835 by Samuel Preston, founder of the *Norwalk Reflector,* as a wedding gift for his daughter Lucy and her husband Frederick Wickham. Here they raised thirteen children. The second floor was used as a printing office for a number of years until too many children forced the newspaper to seek other quarters. It was moved to Case Avenue from its original location on West Main Street and now houses the excellent collections of the Firelands Historical Society, founded in 1857, the second oldest such society in Ohio.

BELOW

The Presbyterians built this house in 1847–48 as a school for girls, called the Presbyterian Female Seminary. It flourished for a number of years and then was sold to H. M. Wooster who converted it into a private residence. Mr. Wooster's daughter married a Boalt and their descendants continued to live in the house until recently. It is now the residence of the curator of the Firelands Historical Society, Norwalk.

Firelands Historical Society

Firelands Historical Society

Map of Lake and Geauga Counties, 1857

OPPOSITE: TOP

The Elwell house, Willoughby, Lake County, one of the very finest examples of Greek Revival, has been attributed to the pioneer master carpenter of Painesville, Jonathan Goldsmith. It was built about 1825–1830.

OPPOSITE: BOTTOM

The Mathews house in Painesville, Lake County, one of the most attractive homes built by Jonathan Goldsmith (1829), is still standing and in good repair, a tribute to an artist and master craftsman of pioneering days. Quite rare are the four pilasters reaching the full height of two stories on the main part of the house, whereas the wings on either side are typical of the period. The doorway is most interesting with its Ionic pillars, unusual carving, and leaded-glass panes. The house was built for Dr. John H. Mathews and his wife Martha Devotion Huntington, daughter of the second governor of Ohio. Saved by a group of citizens, the house is now located on the Lake Erie College campus.

ABOVE

This is another Jonathan Goldsmith home, built in 1820 for Colonel Lemuel G. Storrs and his wife. Purchased in 1855 by Charles A. Avery, it is on its original location on North State Street between Avery Terrace and Rockwood Drive in Painesville. A public reception was given here for Generals Grant, Sherman, and Sheridan at the time General Garfield campaigned for the presidency.

BELOW

Stone Eagle, so called because of the stone eagle on the roof above the main entrance, was built in 1843 by William Hurst on his 600-acre farm near Avon, Lorain County. It is a sturdily constructed home of hand-carved stone blocks, erected over a spring which still provides the household water supply. The interior has a different type of woodwork in each room and eight fireplaces of plain or carved stone. It was restored by Mr. and Mrs. Charles H. Tomes.

Martin Linsey

35

Grace Goulder file

ABOVE

The Edward S. Wells home, Huntington, Lorain County, is the country type of home built by so many of the early settlers. Typical of the popular trend, it is a two-story Greek Revival with a recessed porch. Construction in 1839 is attributed to Reuel Lang, well-known farmer-carpenter of Huntington.

BELOW

Judge Turhand Kirtland, agent for the Connecticut Land Company, and father of the famous naturalist, Jared Potter Kirtland, drew the town of Poland (Mahoning County) as his share of land in the Western Reserve. Here his children and relatives settled, hence we find many of the early homes belonging to Kirtlands. The Mygatt house to the left, showing the Gothic influence, was erected by Eli Mygatt at the time of his marriage to Lois Kirtland in 1831. The Hines home to the right was built by George Kirtland in 1845, and was later occupied by his niece Mrs. Samuel Hines.

George Kirtland Bishc

Carl Boardman Cobb

Elroy Sanford

ABOVE

Henry Mason Boardman built and occupied this house from 1820 to the time of his death in 1846. Devoted to his old homestead in Milford, Connecticut, he spared no labor or expense to create a duplicate in Boardman, Mahoning County, even bringing in sufficient ash lumber by oxcart from Connecticut for the frame of the house. It has the dignity and charm of the fine New England homes.

RIGHT ABOVE

This once lovely Greek Revival homestead in Valley City, Medina County, has been sadly neglected. Unless some steps are taken for its preservation, it will soon disappear from the scene. Built in the 1830's by Sam Arnold, the settlement's master craftsman, it is an excellent example of the dignity incorporated into simple dwellings by the addition of Doric columns supporting a pediment with interesting detail. Craftsman Arnold undoubtedly followed designs in the popular carpenter's manuals. He erected the house for his family. The next generation used it as a tavern and now his grandson, age 80, makes it his home.

RIGHT

Billius Kirtland, son of Turhand Kirtland, built this house in Poland, Mahoning County, in 1830 at the time of his marriage. The name Billius, which has caused much comment, was an honored family name. He was named for his uncle, a well-known doctor in Wallingford, Connecticut. His home, which is one of the loveliest in the Reserve, is threatened with destruction to make room for so-called progress.

Grace Goulder file

OPPOSITE: TOP

This large house was built by Jonathan Hale in 1825 of bricks burned nearby, each reportedly imprinted with a $20 gold piece. This beautiful home with its surrounding 178 acres of meadow and wooded hills in the Cuyahoga Valley, Summit County, together with funds for its maintenance, was willed to the Western Reserve Historical Society by Clara Belle Ritchie, a descendant of Jonathan Hale. It has been restored as a home for gracious living and is now open to the public.

OPPOSITE: BOTTOM

The kitchen or "keeping-room" was an all-purpose room in the early days, much like the big room in the log cabins. Cooking was done over an open fire. Here the family ate and worked and chatted. To the left may be seen the cellar with its original stone wall where fruits, vegetables, meat and other supplies were stored. This section was built into the hillside slope and has no windows.

RIGHT

While the huge Perkins Mansion was being built, Colonel Simon Perkins lived in this Akron home, erected about 1830. Later it housed John Brown's family, while he was in the sheep and wool business with Colonel Perkins. The original home had only four rooms. Two rooms and the porch have been added. It is now owned by the Summit County Historical Society.

BELOW

The Perkins Mansion, Akron, was built in 1831–37 by Colonel Simon Perkins, son of General Perkins of Warren,

All Summit County Historical Society

who helped to found Akron as a key point on the Ohio Canal. With the surrounding beautiful grounds and commanding view of the town from the veranda, it has been and still is a showplace. It is now the home of the Summit County Historical Society and the three floors contain furniture and historical items of Portage Township and Summit County.

Abraham Hine, a native of Milford, Connecticut, purchased 147 acres at $3.00 an acre in Tallmadge, Summit County, and then brought out his wife and their seven children in a "Yankee" wagon pulled by two teams of oxen. They lived in a small cabin on the property for ten years before building this pretentious brick in 1830, the oldest brick house still standing in the town. The bricks were made and burned at the site 243 South Munroe Road.

LEFT BELOW

The present Hudson Library and Historical Society (Summit County) was built in 1830 by Frederick Baldwin, father of Caroline Baldwin Babcock who was born here, and who made it possible for the Historical Society to purchase the home. The architecture shows the influence of Lemuel Porter; the carpenters were his helpers while building the Western Reserve College buildings.

BELOW

Martin Camp, who came to Tallmadge in 1815 from Litchfield County, Connecticut, employed his neighbor Sebbens Saxton to help build this two-story house at 336 North Avenue in 1821, a year before they were both hired as head carpenters to construct the Tallmadge Congregational Church. Some of the detail used in Greek Revival homes may be seen here—the flat planked pediment intended to simulate stone, the slender corner pilasters, and the modillions under the cornice. This is one of the few early homes which has remained much as when it was first built.

The Hudson-Baldwin-Lee home, Hudson, is the oldest house in Summit County. It was built in 1805–06 by David Hudson, founder of Hudson, and is located on Route 91 one-half mile north of the town. The first post office was located here to handle mail brought by stagecoach from Cleveland and Massillon. In the attic, the first Masonic meetings in northern Ohio were held.

The Hosford-Spencer house at 120 Hudson Street, Hudson, Summit County, built in 1832, was at one time the home of the Rev. Henry B. Hosford, minister and professor at Western Reserve College. For years students remembered coming here to take their exams. Although the gambrel-roofed cottage was quite common in Connecticut, it has rarely been seen in the Reserve.

Summit County Historical Society

Henry Mayer

ABOVE

The Allen house, Kinsman, Trumbull County, one of the most beautiful still standing in the Western Reserve, was built in 1821 by Dr. Peter Allen. It was almost lost to posterity when his grandson, Dr. Dudley Allen, removed the fireplace and some of the hand-carved molding in the parlor for his Cleveland home. Luckily, when he died, the Western Reserve Historical Society made arrangements for the return of the missing decorations.

ABOVE

Brownwood, in North Bloomfield, was built in 1815–16 by Ephraim Brown who had purchased 16,000 acres of land in Trumbull County. The facade is most interesting, divided into three panels by four pilasters. The doorway is exceptionally attractive. The house has been in the Brown family for generations.

BELOW

A close-up of the exquisite carving on the Allen House, Kinsman.

ABOVE

The only remaining building of the early days of Warren, Trumbull County, still standing on its original location, is the John Stark Edwards home built in 1807. Upon Edwards' death, it was purchased by the Hon. Thomas Webb and he and his heirs continued to live in the house until recently when it was dedicated as a museum worthy of preservation. The grandson of Jonathan Edwards, John Stark Edwards, was a Yale graduate and the first resident lawyer in the Western Reserve. He was the first recorder for Trumbull County and the first man elected to Congress from the Reserve.

BELOW

This is the old Simon Perkins home which originally stood on the Perkins property on Mahoning Avenue, Warren. It was built before 1816 as it appears on the Louis M. Iddings map of that date. Sometime before 1870 it was moved to East Market Street and restored. A wing and porch were added, but fundamentally it is much as it was when first built.

43

RIGHT

The Kinsman home on Mahoning Avenue in Warren, Trumbull County, is considered another of the most beautiful homes in the Reserve. Built by Isaac Ladd in 1835, it became the home of Frederick Kinsman and his wife, the daughter of Calvin Pease. Here they raised five sons. The house is still in excellent condition and is used today as a courthouse annex.

BELOW

Built by Leicester King in 1828, this house overlooks Monumental Park in Warren, a choice location in its day. It is still standing and in good condition.

Churches

When the Rev. Joseph Badger, one of the earliest missionaries to the Reserve, made his rounds of various settlements in 1801 and 1802, he deplored the lack of piety among the pioneers and the fact that they seemed to "glory in their infidelity."

Although most of the very early settlers came from Connecticut where the Congregational Church played an important part in their lives, they seemed in no apparent rush to establish churches in their new communities. Very few churches were built before 1830, almost 34 years after the surveyors had laid out the townships. There were many reasons for this seeming lack of religion; erecting grist mills, sawmills, dwellings, and raising crops in primitive surroundings demanded their undivided attention.

Contrary to popular opinion, the exodus from Connecticut was not a religious movement but an economic one. The soil of many New England farms had worn out, winters seemed to be getting colder, money was scarce, and providing bare necessities was difficult. Gifts of land in the Firelands and cheap acreage in any township, enhanced by promises of luxuries to come, lured many unsuspecting citizens to isolated settlements where the only emphasis was on survival.

Time brought some semblance of prosperity, and as pressures eased, these pioneers turned to the customs they had left behind. Gradually churches similar to those in New England appeared on village greens in small communities. Religion once again filled an important need in their lives and the church became not only the religious center but also the political and recreational center of the community as it had in their home towns.

As one might expect, membership in the Congregational Church was predominant in the Western Reserve with the Episcopalians and Presbyterians not too far behind. Other denominations such as the Methodists and Baptists had very small congregations in the early 1800's. With the growth of cities after 1850, Catholic and Jewish populations increased. Religious revivals in the East brought two very interesting and dynamic sects to the Reserve: the Shakers, who made a deep impression on Cleveland; and the Mormons in Kirtland, who added a colorful chapter to the history of the area.

In these pages on the early churches, an effort has been made to depict a cross-section of the various denominations and to illustrate the simplicity and original beauty of the better-known structures influenced by the Gothic and Greek Revivals in architecture.

Wherever possible pictures have been grouped to tell a more vivid story: of the Shakers or of the Mormons; of the Boardman Church with its stained-glass window and pewter communion vessels brought with great care in an oxcart from the East; of the beautiful Tallmadge Church and the Rev. David Bacon, who had hoped to build a religious colony exclusively for Congregationalists and Presbyterians; of three churches—Brecksville, Streetsboro, and Twinsburg—so amazingly similar yet built by three individuals at different times in different counties.

The brief captions with each picture are as authentic as exhaustive research can make them. In some cases no records were kept and the only data preserved has been handed down from family to family. There are bound to be some inaccuracies. The important things to remember are that these houses of worship were the cultural and spiritual centers of the communities which surrounded them and that they had a vital part in the development of our most useful citizens for many generations.

ABOVE

Organized in 1834, this was one of the first Universalist churches in northern Ohio. Shortly after organization, members joined the Methodists and the Presbyterians in building a union house of worship until they were able to erect a church of their own in 1847 at Lorain and Butternut Ridge in North Olmsted, Cuyahoga County. Plans are under way to move the church to 5026 Porter Road.

LEFT

Old Stone Church, the first Presbyterian church in Cleveland, dominating the Public Square since its dedication on February 26, 1834, still holds the center of attention in this second edifice with its impressive spire built in 1855.

OPPOSITE: TOP

There was no need for a Catholic church in the Western Reserve until the year 1825 when construction of the Ohio Canal brought an influx of Irish immigrants to Cleveland and Akron. Visiting priests served them until June, 1840, when the small church on Columbus and Girard Streets in the Cleveland flats was dedicated by a Bishop of France, then on a visit to the United States. He named the church Our Lady of the Lake, but over the years the only name by which it was known was St. Mary's on the Flats. It was a frame building of simple construction with four Doric columns. It contained pews and was neatly plastered. It served Catholics of the area until 1852 when St. John's Cathedral was built at Erie and Superior. St. Mary's was then turned over to the German Catholics on the west side, who had long been wanting a church of their own.

About 1845 Father Peter McLaughlin realized that St. Mary's-on-the-Flats could not take care of the growing Catholic population in Cleveland. With unusual foresight he purchased land on Erie Street for a future church in the face of great criticism because it was on the eastern outskirts of the city. It was feared no one would travel that far to attend Mass. Three years later the corner stone was laid for St. John's Cathedral. It was completed November 7, 1852, the second Catholic church in the city. The Cathedral was a sturdy brick building 170 x 75 ft, styled along French Gothic lines. It could comfortably accommodate 900 persons.

The Anshe Chesed Jewish congregation established the first synagogue in Cleveland in 1846 on Eagle Street. In 1850 the congregation split over differences in the form of worship and doctrine. The original church eventually became the Fairmount Temple. The offshoot, known as the Tifereth Israel Congregation, grew in popularity because of its liberal attitude. It sponsored educational and social activities as well as religious and soon was recognized as the first "Open Temple." It is now known as The Temple at University Circle. Among the very notable early Jews in the congregation was Dr. Daniel Peixotto, a native of the West Indies and a graduate of Columbia University. He came to Cleveland in 1835 and was one of the prominent doctors chosen for the teaching staff of Willoughby Medical College at the time of its organization. Another prominent Jew of those early days was Isadore Kalisch who came from Bavaria in 1849 and served as the first Rabbi of the Temple on Huron Road.

Catholic Universe Bulletin

Scovill Avenue Temple, Semi-Centennial Book, 1896

Catholic Universe Bulletin

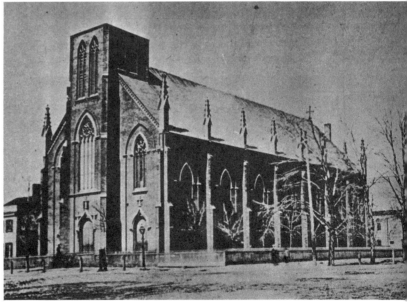

47

St. John's Historic Episcopal Church on Church Avenue is considered the oldest church in Greater Cleveland still standing on its original site. The first service was held in Phineas Shepherd's cabin on November 9, 1816, but the cornerstone for the building was not laid until July 2, 1836. That year on October 22 a prominent wedding was held at the church uniting Daniel Rhodes and Sophia Lord Russell. A stained-glass window commemorates the event. They became the parents of famous children: Mrs. Mark Hanna, Robert Rhodes, and James Ford Rhodes. The church was an escape station for runaway slaves who hid in the belfry and watched boats coming across Lake Erie to carry them to Canada and freedom.

RIGHT BELOW
The little Episcopal church in Peninsula, Summit County, built and endowed in 1835 by Harmon Bronson, is one of the landmarks of early canal days, when the town boomed with shipping and trade, as a stop on the Ohio Canal. Practically all traces of that busy time have been erased but the little church stands firm despite the controversy of whether it should be moved to the Hale Farm or stay on its original foundation. Its architecture is similar to many of the community churches of that era. This one has the Gothic windows and boxy tower. This detail of a water color by the late William Sommer shows the church steeple as it was before some of the structure was removed.

OPPOSITE
A typical New England church on the village green, this Congregational church in Tallmadge, Summit County, is still considered an architectural gem. Built 1821–1825 by Lemuel Porter, master craftsman and architect recently arrived from Connecticut, it stands as a symbol of the early religious life in the Western Reserve.

Western Reserve Historical Society

Robert Bordner

48

ABOVE

This charming painting of Col. Benjamin Tallmadge and his young son William, by the famous artist Ralph Earl, hangs in the Historical Museum in Litchfield, Connecticut. It is a gentle reminder to those in the Reserve of the close connections we have had with the mother colony, Connecticut. A revolutionary soldier and keen business man, Tallmadge speculated in many ventures and made quite a fortune buying and selling land in several states. He expressed no interest in coming to the Western Reserve, yet became a large landowner through mortgages which had fallen in arrears; six thousand acres were in the vicinity of Tallmadge. The Rev. David Bacon, who had hoped to make this a religious colony, chose the name Tallmadge in honor of the man who owned the land and who was also a devout member of his own Congregational church.

RIGHT ABOVE

Although the township of Tallmadge had been assigned to purchasers in 1798, it was not laid out until nine years later when the Rev. David Bacon, a former missionary to the Reserve, conceived the idea of establishing a partially communal religious colony. He purchased on a time-payment plan most of the township at $1.50 an acre to be resold to his parishioners—professing Congregationalists and Presbyterians. His plan of eight roads radiating from a village square was carried out, homes were built and all went well for a while, but differences of opinion on financial and religious issues caused a rift. After a five-year struggle Bacon admitted defeat and took his family back East. The unsold lots were returned to the original owners.

50

OPPOSITE

St. James Episcopal Church in Boardman, Mahoning County, is the oldest Episcopal church in the Western Reserve, having been organized in 1809 at a meeting conducted by Judge Turhand Kirtland. It took twenty years to get a church building. It was dedicated in 1829 by Bishop Philander Chase as the parish of Poland, Boardman, and Canfield. The Boardman family, staunch supporters of the church and original owners of the township, had strong ties with their eastern home in New Milford, Connecticut. Their Reserve home was an almost identical reproduction of the old homestead.

ABOVE

Sarah Hall Benham, 1796–1870, the daughter of a minister, came on the long trek west in 1819 as the bride of Henry Mason Boardman, son of a prosperous merchant in New Milford, Connecticut. More fortunate than most of the emigrants, they drove on this bridal trip in a carriage drawn by two horses. An oxcart followed with the necessities of life. Both Sarah and Henry, although accustomed to a more leisurely and cultured way of life, tackled pioneer living with great vigor and enthusiasm, he as a farmer and she as a housewife. They both took an important part in the religious and civic life of the town of Boardman.

RIGHT ABOVE

First communion vessels, made of pewter, and the Bible, dated 1831, were brought to St. James Episcopal Church by oxcart from New Milford, Connecticut, by the Henry Mason Boardmans. The stained glass window, shown at right, was brought at the same time.

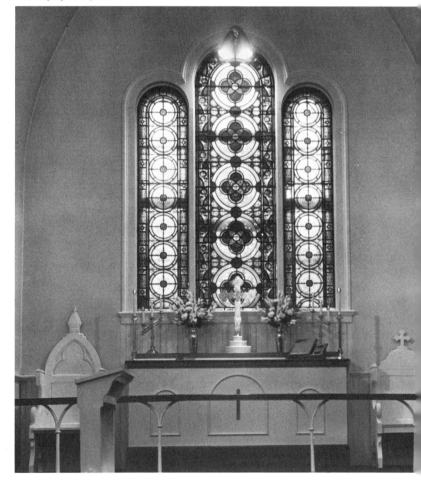

51

St. Peter's Episcopal Church in Ashtabula, Ashtabula County, was organized in 1816. It was the first church to have weekly communion west of the Allegheny Mountains. The cornerstone for the new church was laid in 1829 and was consecrated by Bishop Philander Chase. The Rev. Joseph Badger's son-in-law, John Hall, was rector of this church several times.

The Rev. Joseph Badger, a Congregational minister, had come to the Western Reserve as the first missionary late in 1800. He traveled on horseback, preaching and praying with families and groups assembled to hear him. He lodged with Lorenzo Carter in Cleveland on August 18th. In October he was in Austinburg organizing the first Congregational church. After a time, his work was directed to the Indians along the Maumee River.

The South Ridge Baptist Church, south of Conneaut on State Route 7, Ashtabula County, was erected in 1832. Five years later at a general conference of Free Will Baptists the congregation entertained representatives from Maine to Wisconsin and as far south as the Carolinas. The Free Will Baptists eventually merged with the Baptists.

Christ Episcopal Church at Windsor Mills, Ashtabula County, was authentically restored in 1961, which earned for it an award from the American Institute of Architects, Cleveland Chapter. It was built in 1832 and dedicated two years later. Like the Claridon Church on the same highway, it has Gothic windows and square boxes composing the tower. In lieu of a steeple there are five little peaks, one in the center and four at the corners.

The Claridon Church, Geauga County, is another of a number of churches organized as Presbyterian which later became Congregational. It was built in 1831 and dedicated the following year. The backs of all the pews are said to have been made from one large whitewood tree. The church has an interesting cornice, double doors, Gothic windows, and a boxy tower.

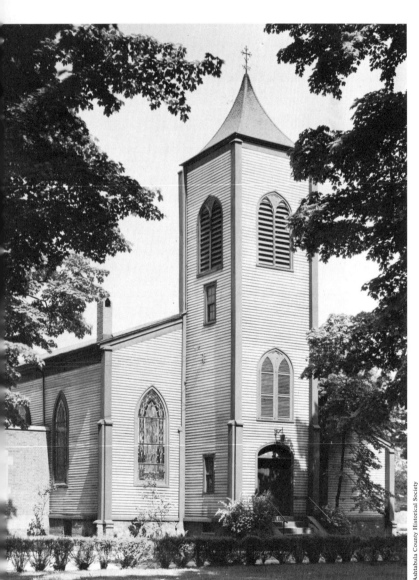

Ashtabula County Historical Society

Western Reserve Historical Society

52

St. Christopher's By-The-River, Episcopal, was originally a Methodist church. It was built about 1853 on land provided by Holsey Gates, who also paid a good share of the building costs. Lumber for the church was cut in his mill. The town, Gates Mills, Cuyahoga County, was named for him.

Freedom Congregational Church, Portage County, is outstanding because of its massive Greek pillars at the entrance. Its boxy tower, however, seems to dwarf the first impression of height and strength. The church was built in 1845 for $3,000. Here again there was controversy about the denomination. It was organized in 1828 as Presbyterian, but later became Congregational.

Grace Goulder

LEFT BELOW

The Congregational Church (now United Church of Christ), facing the green in Twinsburg, Summit County, was built in 1848 at a cost of $3,200. According to architect Robert C. Gaede, "It is a timeless building, a charming bit of Greek Revival, Doric order."

RIGHT BELOW

Built in 1840, the Episcopal Church, Wadsworth, Medina County, is considered a good example of Greek Revival with its low pediment supporting massive columns. It has been the scene of worship for several denominations, the Congregationalists, Mennonites, and recently the Episcopalians.

Grace Goulder photograph

Grace Goulder file

Grace Goulder file

55

The Brecksville Congregational Church, Cuyahoga County, was erected in 1844 by Simeon C. Porter, son of Lemuel Porter who had built the Tallmadge Church. Under leadership of the first minister, Newton Barrett, funds for the building were raised by sale of pews, front pews $100 and center $50. The Articles of Regulation of this Congregational church considered it a violation of Christian duty to collect hay or grain on the Sabbath or even to visit friends except in cases of illness.

RIGHT BELOW
Streetsboro Methodist Church in Portage County was built in 1851 by James Clark. At the time of its organization in 1833 the congregation was Baptist instead of the usual Congregational-Presbyterian merger. The Methodists took over late in the 1800's. Typical of the average New England church in its simplicity and beauty of line, it has long been a landmark of Portage County. Set back from Route 14 at its intersection with Route 43, it is also visible on Route 303.

OPPOSITE: LEFT ABOVE
Begun in 1838, the Congregational Church at Atwater, Portage County, was dedicated November 7, 1841. It is thought that the steeple was added later. The combination of the pointed windows, typical of the Gothic influence, and the pure classicism of the portico and the steeple is rather unusual, but does not detract from the beauty of the church, which is considered one of the finest in the Reserve.

OPPOSITE: RIGHT ABOVE
Built by the Presbyterians of Elyria (Lorain County) in 1848, this church eventually became the First Congregational. It was considered one of the finest Gothic-type structures in Ohio.

OPPOSITE: LEFT BELOW
The Kinsman Congregational Church, Trumbull County, built about 1832, is supposedly a replica of the Old North Church in New Haven. The Kinsman family engaged a master builder named Willie Smith and his co-workers, all recently arrived from Connecticut, to erect the church and several houses.

OPPOSITE: RIGHT BELOW
The Rev. John Ingersoll, noted for his fiery anti-slavery sermons, drew crowds to the Presbyterian Church in Rome, Ashtabula County, at a time when the abolition movement was gaining favor in the north.

Mike Bryan, Brecksville

Grace Goulder file

THE MORMONS

BELOW

The unique Mormon Temple in Kirtland, Lake County, showing the unmistakable influence of the Gothic and Greek Revival architecture so prevalent in the Reserve in the early part of the nineteenth century, was completed in 1836 after three years of labor and prayer. It is a memorial to the founder Joseph Smith, who claimed that God had revealed to him alone, on plates of gold, the lost scriptural record of Mormon. After emigrating from Palmyra, New York, he established a colony of about 200 believers in Kirtland and soon thereafter directed the design and construction of this large stone temple, covered with stucco, situated on a hill and visible for miles around. Each man donated one day of work each

week either to haul stones from a nearby quarry or do some of the elaborate wood carving on the interior. Each day Joseph Smith received spiritual visions of how to proceed with the construction of the temple. He was not destined to enjoy his church, for due to financial troubles and the banking panic of 1837 he was forced to flee. After his death, one branch of the church accepted the leadership of Brigham Young who led them to Utah. The remaining few in the Kirtland church continued the tradition of Joseph Smith, eventually claiming title to the Temple under a new name, the Reorganized Church of Jesus Christ of the Latter Day Saints. It still holds services today.

OPPOSITE: TOP
The big central window with its elliptical arch dominates the interior of the Mormon Temple. Skilled workmanship is displayed in the twelve pulpits constructed in four tiers of three pulpits each, and in the elaborate carving around the windows and above the columns.

Shaker Historical Society

THE SHAKERS

RIGHT TOP
In 1822 the North Union Society of Shakers was established by Ralph Russell, an early pioneer of Warrensville, who had recently been converted. Through his earnestness and effective persuasion, members of his large family joined the movement and won many more converts until in 1851 there was a thriving settlement with 200 members in three communal groups called "families" in the area around the present Shaker Boulevard and Lee Road, Cuyahoga County.

Men and women, living in separate sections of the same dormitories, led celibate lives. All their personal property and even their children had been turned over to the sect when they joined. In the very early days they managed to be self-sufficient, erecting a grist and saw mill, building dwellings, raising their own food, and making all necessary clothing. Later on during their more prosperous days they also served the surrounding community by establishing a woolen factory, a tannery, a woodenware factory, a linseed oil mill, and a broom factory. The Shakers believed in a rigid, simple life and in doing each task to the best of one's ability. Their orderly habits, their industry, and their thrift were greatly admired by the early settlers. Decline of the Society occurred when it could no longer compete with manufactured goods from Cleveland and when the older members died. It was dissolved in 1889.

RIGHT BOTTOM
In 1843 a new grist mill, the only stone building in the colony of Shakers, was built near the stone quarry on the north side of the creek. On the south end it was four stories high, a monument of solid masonry, its workmanship pronounced the finest in Ohio. This copy was made from an etching by A. M. Willard, the famous artist.

Western Reserve Historical Society

59

LEFT

The Shaker meeting house, located near the Shaker Center Family Dwelling, was dedicated November 29, 1849. Here the Shakers held their religious services, the men sitting in one section, the women in another. Part of the service was a slow march around the meeting hall. After long periods of walking, as weariness set in, the shaking would begin, hence the name of Shakers.

BELOW

The Mill or North Family House was built in 1838 near Coventry Road and the west end of the lower lake in Shaker Heights. At the right of the home is the cheese house and at the left is the spring house and the wash house. At the extreme left across the bridge and over the creek are the horse barns and wagon sheds. The wide road is the present Coventry Road. The family consisted of about fifty members. They looked after the grist mill, saw mill, and stone quarry and did some farming.

Valley of God's Pleasure by Caroline B. Piercy

Education

Many of the early settlers came from cultured communities in Connecticut. They were greatly distressed when they realized that their children would receive no education unless they, themselves, provided it. Wherever a few families were within walking distance of each other an effort was made to establish a school in one corner of a cabin where children could gather for a few hours of instruction in the three "R's."

A teacher's only qualification was a willingness to teach and keep discipline; his only equipment a wooden paddle with the alphabet on one side and the multiplication table on the other. Soon these makeshift classrooms were replaced by better accommodations in one-room schoolhouses built of logs, stone, or the familiar red brick. As communities were able to pay their teachers a small sum, they demanded more qualifications than a mere knowledge of the three 'R's," the most important being "a good moral character."

As the demand for higher education increased, academies and colleges were organized and fine structures erected. Colleges were patterned in both curricula and architecture after eastern colleges. Oberlin was the first college to admit women; and Willoughby, later Lake Erie Seminary, pioneered in education exclusively for women. The need for doctors encouraged the formation of Willoughby Medical College in 1834; and in 1845 Western Reserve College at Hudson erected a medical building in Cleveland.

Education in the Reserve made great strides from the crude beginnings in 1800. By 1860 anyone eager to learn could secure a secondary or college education without traveling great distances to the East.

A typical log schoolhouse interior, sketched by Edwin Tunis, serves to illustrate the first log schoolhouse in the Reserve at Warren, 1801. It had one door and windows covered with greased paper. Pupils sat on rough-cut benches. A year earlier Sarah Doan conducted classes in her home in Newburgh near Cleveland. Her teaching materials consisted of a wooden paddle with the alphabet on one side and the multiplication table on the other. Books and paper were very scarce.

Frontier Living by Edwin Tunis, World Publishing

Grace Goulder file

ABOVE
The contract for building this stone schoolhouse at Concord, Painesville-Chardon Road, Lake County, was given to James McEuen, November 23, 1840. He finished it August 1, 1841, and his bill was the large sum of $200.

LEFT
Little Red Schoolhouse, Oberlin, Lorain County. The one-room little red schoolhouse was a familiar landmark in nearly every small community in the 1840's and 1850's. A teacher was engaged to dispense reading, writing, and arithmetic to all ages. Wages amounted to very little cash plus room and board in a student's home. One specific requirement for a teacher was that he or she be of good moral character.

OPPOSITE: TOP
The Old Stone Schoolhouse in Akron is a small, one-room building, approximately 32 x 38 feet, constructed of blocks of gray sandstone taken from nearby quarries. It is located at 299 South Broadway on the site of the first public school in the area. It is the oldest school building still standing and was probably built before 1840. It was

62

in use when Akron's first Board of Education approved passage of the Graded School Plan in 1847, which became the pattern for the graded school law for Ohio. It is now the property of the Summit County Historical Society. Plans are under way for its restoration.

RIGHT

A slab schoolhouse of small dimensions, but sufficient for the time, was erected in Chagrin Falls, Cuyahoga County, as early as the summer of 1835 on the slope of the hill, now the west side of Main Street opposite Triangle Park. Miss Almeda Vincent, daughter of the first physician in the community, was the first teacher. The scholars rambled in the woods or skated on the frozen overflow of the creek at recess and noontime. Some of these scholars were the children of Henry Church, Sr., one of the first settlers. His home, with his blacksmith shop beside it, stood opposite the school. His oldest son, Henry Church, Jr., one of the first children born in the village, sketched this school as he remembered it. He gained quite a reputation in the Cleveland area as a sculptor for his carvings on Squaw Rock.

63

BELOW

At 9 o'clock on a dark night in February, 1809, the John Wright family with their ox teams, wagons, and possessions reached Tallmadge, Summit County, the forest resounding with hymns as they came. John Wright, Jr., and his wife Saloma, natives of Windsor, Connecticut, both came from musical families and their sheer joy in singing old familiar tunes inspired the early settlers to join in. Only a few months after their arrival John Wright was engaged to teach the first singing school in the Reserve. Below is a transcription of the original singing school contract between John Wright and his pupils.

"WE, the subscribers being desirous of having a Singing School in the Town of Talmadge to be kept One Night at the Center and One Night at the schoolhouse in the West Settlement of said Talmadge in each and every week successively for three months we the subscribers therefore promise by these presents to pay Mr. John Wright Jr. One Dollar for every scholar sat against our Respective Names to be paid in good Merchantable Grain at the expiration of three months for his services in teaching said school. December 10th 1809."

Platt R. Spencer, uneducated and brought up in dire poverty, became the world's foremost penman. Obsessed with the desire to write at a time when even a sheet of paper was a luxury, he practiced his art in the sand, the snow, or upon birch bark. He invented the legible yet beautiful penmanship known everywhere as Spencerian writing.

In 1853 Platt R. Spencer built a log seminary on Jericho Road, Geneva, Ashtabula County, where he conducted summer institutes for writing teachers. For many years his system became the foundation of writing in schools across the country.

Western Reserve Historical Society

Grace Goulder file

BELOW

This in the scene that greeted Henry Howe, Ohio's famous chronicler, when he visited Western Reserve College in Hudson, Summit County, in 1846. The buildings of brick are similar to Yale, although not exact reproductions. Most of them were built by Lemuel Porter and his son Simeon. In this sketch are left to right: Professors House, the Athenaeum, President's House, Divinity Hall, Chapel, Middle Hall, South Hall, Loomis Observatory.

LEFT

Western Reserve College was granted a charter in 1826. In April of that year the cornerstone of Middle College was laid. It was the first building of the proud new "Yale of the West" located in a typical New England setting. A theology department was established in 1830, this chapel built in 1836, and a chemistry department installed in 1837. This was a progressive college, admitting students of any race, creed, or color; and although claiming to be non-sectarian, chapel attendance was required and the Sabbath religiously observed.

OPPOSITE: TOP LEFT

David Hudson (1761–1836), like his illustrious ancestor Hendrik Hudson, was filled with the spirit of adventure which brought him from Goshen, Connecticut, to the Western Reserve in 1799 to explore the land he had purchased at 34¢ an acre. The following year he brought his wife, six children, hired help, and friends to form a settlement, named Hudson in his honor. By fall another daughter was added to the family, the first white child born in Summit County. In 1806 he moved his family from a log cabin to a large frame house, still standing on Route 91, its exterior, including the old fence, unchanged. He was appointed a justice of the peace by Governor St. Clair, a position he held for twenty-five years. He solicited the earliest funds, donating $2,000 of his own for the establishment of Western Reserve College of which he was a founder and trustee. After his death, his heirs gave about seventeen acres of land for campus purposes.

66

ABOVE

Loomis Observatory of Western Reserve College was built in 1838, the first west of the Allegheny Mountains. Still standing, it is the second oldest on the American continent. Hopkins Observatory at Williams College is slightly older. It was named for Elias Loomis, astronomy professor, under whose direction the building was erected.

BELOW

President's House on the campus of Western Reserve College was built for the president and the professor of theology. The first three presidents, Charles B. Storrs, George E. Pierce, and Henry L. Hitchcock, lived in the north half.

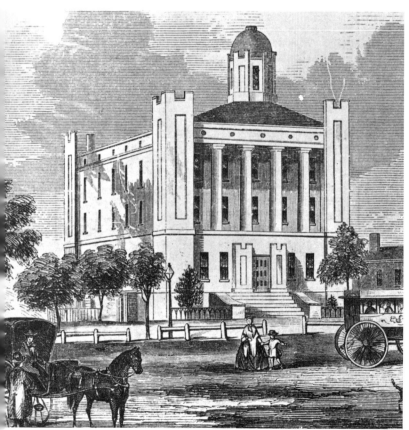

LEFT ABOVE

The Nutting House, at 79 Hudson Street, Hudson, was built in 1831 by Rufus Nutting, first professor of languages at Western Reserve College. It has a most unusual doorway, undoubtedly the work of an inspired local carpenter.

LEFT BELOW

The Cleveland Medical College, a part of Western Reserve College, was built in 1845 at the corner of St. Clair and Erie Street. It was a four-and-a-half-story structure with an imposing entrance.

OPPOSITE: TOP LEFT

Harvey Rice (1800–1891) came from Massachusetts to Cleveland at the age of twenty-four in September, 1824, his most precious possessions a letter of recommendation and his A.B. diploma written in Latin from Williams College. The second day after his arrival he was hired as classical teacher and principal of the Cleveland Academy. While still teaching, he studied law under Reuben Wood and two years later entered political life. He served in many capacities: as Justice of the Peace, Representative to the State Legislature, clerk of the Common Pleas Court, and as the first Democrat sent to the legislature from Cuyahoga County. He was appointed agent for the sale of Western Reserve school lands in 1830.

He made his greatest impression after his election to the State Senate in 1851 when he introduced a bill on which our free school system is based. It became law and a model for other states. He was also concerned with legislation for the prevention of crime and the reformation of criminals. He was the author of a number of books and scholarly papers and the first president of the Early Settlers Association. In 1857 he introduced legislation in Cleveland Council and later headed the committee responsible for the erection of the Perry Monument.

OPPOSITE: TOP RIGHT

These are the cards of admission used by G. Anderson Hull to attend lectures and classes, 1845–46, in the Medical Department of Western Reserve College.

OPPOSITE: BOTTOM LEFT

The Cleveland Academy opened in 1822 on the north side of St. Clair near Bank Street. A good education could be secured over a twelve-week period for only $4.00. The course included reading, spelling, writing, grammar, geography, Greek, Latin, and higher mathematics. The two-story brick building had a handsome spire and a bell tower.

OPPOSITE: BOTTOM RIGHT

A teacher's certificate was issued by a board of examiners in Cuyahoga County to A. W. Ingalls stating that he is qualified to teach reading, writing, arithmetic, geography, grammar, botany, philosophy, and algebra and that he sustains a good moral character. His own signature, which is identical with the handwriting on the certificate, is found among the signers of the examination, issued the 31st of October, 1838.

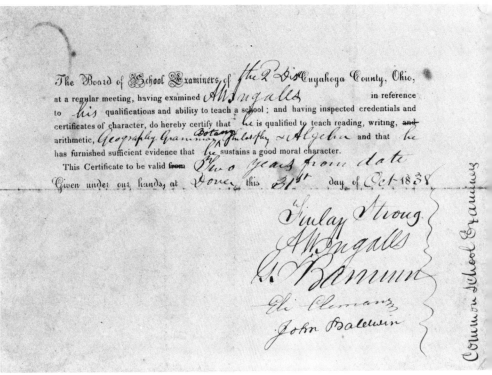

69

ABOVE

The town of Oberlin in Lorain County and its college were founded in 1833 and named for John Oberlin, an Alsatian pastor and philanthropist who had never visited the United States and was unaware that a college would be named for him. He died in Switzerland seven years before the college was founded. Oberlin was the first college in the country to admit women on the same status as men. It was a hotbed for the abolitionist movement and soon became a famous station in the Underground Railroad. In this sketch drawn by Henry Howe in 1846 are, left to right: Oberlin Hall, Ladies' Hall, Colonial and Tappan Halls, and the Presbyterian Church.

TOP LEFT

The Big Tent was brought from New York in 1835 by Oberlin President Finney to be used for Commencement and other large meetings until the First Church was built. It was one hundred feet in diameter and enclosed 3,000 people. During 1842 and 1843 it was used for Sabbath services. It was later purchased by an anti-slavery society and used throughout the country for mass meetings.

BOTTOM LEFT

Many important events took place in the shadow of Oberlin's Historic Elm.

OPPOSITE: TOP LEFT

Oberlin College established a branch Manual Labor Institute in 1836 on the 300-acre Burrell farm in Sheffield, Lorain County. Students planted 17,500 mulberry trees as part of a project to study silkworm culture. Classes were held in the brick home built about 1820 by Sheffield's earliest pioneer, Jabez Burrell. The mulberries hardly had a chance to mature before the venture was abandoned. However, Oberlin kept in touch with the Burrells, ardent sympathizers of the abolition movement. Familiar with the home and its easy access to the lake, faculty and students aided escaping slaves to seek its shelter as the last stop on the road to Canada. Descendants of Jabez Burrell still live in the old homestead.

70

Oberliniana Jubilee Volume

TOP RIGHT

Caroline Mary Rudd of Huntington, Connecticut, who enrolled in Oberlin in 1837 was one of the first three women graduates in the first co-educational college in the country. She received her A.B. in 1841.

ABOVE

Colonial Hall, built in 1835, stood at the corner of College and Professor Streets. It was a three-story frame building containing the chapel, classrooms, and dormitories for 44 students.

RIGHT

The First Church, built in 1843 at a cost of $12,000, could seat 1800, filling a great need for a college auditorium.

71

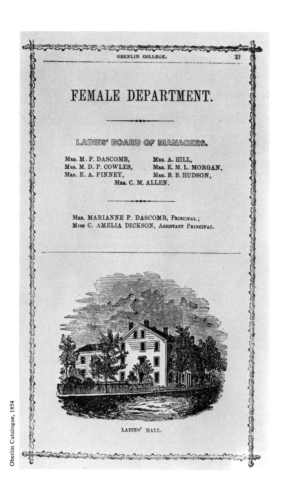

FEMALE DEPARTMENT.

LADIES' BOARD OF MANAGERS.

Mrs. M. P. DASCOMB,   Mrs. A. HILL,
Mrs. M. D. P. COWLES,   Mrs. E. M. L. MORGAN,
Mrs. E. A. FINNEY,   Mrs. B. B. HUDSON,
Mrs. C. M. ALLEN.

Mrs. MARIANNE P. DASCOMB, Principal;
Miss C. AMELIA DICKSON, Assistant Principal.

LADIES' HALL.

Oberlin Catalogue, 1854

LEFT
Ladies' Hall was the Female Department of Oberlin College. The department had its own female principal and Ladies' Board of Managers. Built in 1835, it served as dormitory for women and dining hall. The third floor was used as a club room for literary and religious debates.

BELOW
Tappan Hall, Oberlin College, was named for Arthur Tappan of New York, a staunch abolitionist and a generous donor to the college funds. This was the first hall, built in 1835.

OPPOSITE: TOP LEFT
These Oberlin students were candidates for the Bachelor's Degree in 1855.

OPPOSITE: TOP RIGHT
The first chemistry laboratory at Oberlin was known as Dr. Dascomb's lab.

OPPOSITE: BOTTOM
By the year 1830 the people of Milan, Erie County, decided they needed a school of higher learning. Residents and the clergy pooled their resources and then started an active campaign to raise funds for the Huron Institute, or the Milan Academy as it was sometimes called. The building was completed by 1832 and was in operation a year before Oberlin College. After 1858 it was known as the Western Reserve Normal School and it continued as such for the next 31 years.

Oberlin College Library

Oberlin College Library

Oberlin College Library

73

LEFT

John Baldwin, one of the sturdiest pioneers in the Reserve, settled in Berea, Cuyahoga County, with his bride Mary in 1828, and together they created major changes in the settlement. Their home was the first to be raised without the benefit of liquor. In this house were held the first town meeting, and the first Church and Sunday School sessions. The first grindstone was hewn in the basement, and an occasional slave was given food and lodging. With a fortune accumulated from the manufacture of grindstones he paid his debts and founded Baldwin Institute in 1845. Later, in the true pioneering spirit, he founded a town and university in Kansas, a school in Louisiana, and two high schools in Bangalore, India.

BELOW

In 1838 John Baldwin gave an examination in spelling, reading, writing, and arithmetic to Miss Cora Bradford and found her qualified to teach school in Olmsted. He was also satisfied that she had a good moral character.

BOTTOM

An early view of the Baldwin Institute campus shows the First Methodist Church at the left. Two of the earliest buildings are shown at the right, called North and South Halls.

ABOVE

A page from the catalogue of the Officers and Students of Baldwin Institute for the term ending June 30, 1848, indicates the low fees and stringent rules which students were required to observe.

BELOW

The Grand River Institute, chartered in 1831 as the Ashtabula County School of Science and Industry, was originally located at Mechanicsburg. In 1835, through a request and a grant of $25,000 from Joab Austin, it was moved to Austinburg. It was one of the first academies to admit women.

BELOW

Erected about 1820, this house served as an academy in Tallmadge, Summit County. Elizur Wright was instructor, followed by Ephraim T. Sturtevant who purchased this building, moved it on to his land, and continued to operate the school. It is still in the same location, known as the oldest frame building in the town.

LEFT

Lake Erie College, Painesville, was built in 1857–59, shortly after the Willoughby Female Seminary burned and Lake County could offer no higher education for young ladies. This original building housed classrooms and living quarters for students and faculty. It was constructed under the supervision of architect Charles Wallace Heard, an apprentice under Jonathan Goldsmith and later a partner of Simeon Porter, both master craftsmen of the early 1800's. The Seminary, as it was called in the early days, was modeled after Mt. Holyoke College; its first faculty was made up of six graduates of that eastern school, only two of whom had any teaching experience.

BELOW

Chester Seminary in Chesterland, Geauga County, was established in 1842 and this building erected the following year. It was here James A. Garfield received his religious training and where he met Lucretia Rudolph, who later became his wife.

76

This photograph of a Greek class at Hiram College, Lake County, was taken April 24, 1853, by A. S. Robbins. Seated, left to right (front row): Philip Burns, Jennie Gardner, Lucretia Rudolph, James A. Garfield; (back row): E. S. Pike, Joseph King, George O'Connor, Sterling McBride. Note that James Garfield and Lucretia Rudolph studied Greek in the same class at Hiram.

BELOW

The Arkites were a group of young men, mainly interested in the collection and study of natural history specimens, who gathered in a one-story building called the Ark at the northeast corner of Cleveland's Public Square for discussion and good fellowship. This informal group was painted in 1858 by Julius Gollman, a German artist. They are, from left to right: Dr. Elisha Sterling, Captain Benjamin Stanard, James J. Tracy, William Case (holding paper), Dr. Alleyn Maynard (standing), Bushnell White, David W. Cross (hand on knee), Leonard Case, Edward A. Scovill, George A. Stanley (tall hat), Col. Stoughton Bliss (foreground), Rufus K. Winslow, John Coon, and Henry G. Abbey (standing).

Lake County Historical Society

Western Reserve Historical Society

Jared Potter Kirtland (1793–1877), a man of great stature both physically and mentally, has left a deep impression on the Western Reserve. As an outstanding physician, top-ranking naturalist, and member of the Ohio Legislature for three terms, he played an important part in the days of the early settlements. He was one of the founders of the Medical School of Western Reserve University. The Cleveland Museum of Natural History is the culmination of his initial interest in organizing a group of naturalists in Cleveland, known as the Arkites. During 1837, while in charge of a zoological research project for the State of Ohio, he identified 585 vertebrates, and his report included a catalogue of birds, reptiles, fishes, mollusks, and insects—the most complete list ever made for this section of the country. His insatiable desire to experiment, his earnestness and unselfish willingness to share his vast knowledge, won for him unstinting praise from all who knew him. His name has been memorialized at the Cleveland Museum of Natural History, at the Medical School of Western Reserve University, and in Lakewood where he spent the greater part of his life. Although his famous garden in Lakewood is gone, Kirtland Library in the Oldest Stone House and Kirtland Lane are reminders of his share in the community.

No one in the Western Reserve contributed more to the study of its geology than Charles Whittlesey (1808–1886). Born in Connecticut, he came with his parents to Tallmadge at the age of five. He received his higher education at West Point, graduating with honors in 1831. After service in the Black Hawk War he opened a law office in Cleveland and at the same time became part-owner and co-editor of *The Whig and Herald*. From 1837–1839 he was appointed assistant geologist of the Ohio Survey, and it was in this field he found his greatest interest. An earnest and thorough student, he made an extensive study of the Indian mounds of Ohio, published many scientific papers, a valuable *Early History of Cleveland,* and gave free public lectures on the mineral resources of Ohio and Michigan. He was largely responsible for the discovery and development of the great iron and copper regions of Lake Superior. His title of Colonel was earned during the Civil War. Organizer and first president of the Western Reserve Historical Society, he encouraged the preservation of many historical and geological documents which might otherwise have been lost, thereby making Cleveland the richest reservoir of research in northern Ohio.

Western Reserve University Medical School

Western Reserve Historical Society

Recreation and the Arts

Pleasures in the early days of the settlements were few and simple, involving practically no expense, such as walks down lover's lane or along the lake and streams. Husking and quilting bees made farm tasks lighter, whereas the singing festivals, spelling bees, and literary societies provided wholesome entertainment. Making maple sugar was fun for the entire family. Highlights of the year were dances and balls, scheduled, as a rule, for Independence Day and Christmas. These were gay affairs when trunks were ransacked for bits of finery brought from the East, and when men were as fastidious about their dress as women. Occasionally a circus came to town with parades of strange animals, the fat lady, the thin man, perhaps a fire eater or Siamese twins.

The early nineteenth century, before the invention of photography, was a period of flourishing "primitive" art in the Western Reserve. Itinerant sign and barn painters discovered they could paint convincing scenes and people. Little children, important officials, and entire families had their portraits painted. Charming primitive paintings, despite their lack of sophistication, found prominent places in many homes. The desire to decorate barren walls and keep hands busy resulted in an abundance of samplers, frakturs, and intricate wreaths made of hair or feathers.

Interest in art, music, and the theater increased as more talent became available. Beginning in the mid-fifties, larger towns were attracting some of the best entertainment the country could offer. Sandusky became the location of a nationally-renowned Art and Literary Association with a membership of over 22,000, which stimulated interest in good literature and brought to the Reserve outstanding works of art for annual exhibition and distribution.

Although the Reserve had produced art that reflected the simple life, by mid-century people were seeking more sophisticated art and entertainment.

The Fourth of July Ball in 1801 at Carter's Tavern, Cleveland, was an event often recounted by the early settlers who participated. A most vivid description has been preserved by Gilman Bryant, who at the age of seventeen took Miss Doan, then fourteen, to this gay affair. He wore a gingham suit, a good wool hat, and a pair of brogans. His hair was queued with one and a half yards of black ribbon and sprinkled with flour. Gilman lived near the Carters at the mouth of the Cuyahoga, but in order to escort Miss Doan he had to ride an old horse almost five miles east to Doan's Corners. She mounted on behind him and they had a fine time.

Recollections by S. G. Goodrich

Harley W. Hoffman

Mrs. Donald C. Stem

Independence Ball.

The coffee-pot will be boiling, boys;
You need not doubt or fear,
Thirty-five setts can dance at once,
And more if they are here,
A dining room one hundred feet—
In this I am sincere ;
And "fixings" enough to back it up,
Or Stocking won't be here.

Your Company

Is respectfully solicited at the **"Mammoth Hall"** of
D. W. STOCKING, in Chardon, on Thursday, July 4th, 1850,
at 1 o'clock P. M.

Room Managers,
A. L. SMITH,   A. SCOTT,   A. PHELPS, Jr.

MANAGERS.

W. E. SMITH, Chardon,	T. G. WRIGHT, Mantua.
R. DARLING, Painesville.	R GILCHRIST, do.
N. ANDREWS, Newbury.	C. SHAW, Chester.
R. CARVER, Chardon.	H. HOLMES, Kirtland.
D. PULSIPHER, Newbury.	G. HOLMES, Mayfield.
E. HODGE, Claridon,	J. CONDIT, Euclid.
S. CHURCH, Huntsburg,	D. A. VAN BROCHER, Wil'by.
C. CLEVELAND, Centreville,	H. HIGLEY, Windsor,
D. A. BAXTER, Burton,	M. D. PHELPS, Bloomfield,
C. LACE, Leroy,	F. WILLIAMS, Parkman.
W. EVANS, Montville,	H. BEECHER, Shalersville.
L. A. FOOT, Shalersville,	S. SCOTT, Chagrin Falls.
J. MOORE, Munson,	J. T. ROBERTS, Unionville.
A. MOFFET, Middlefield,	O. ROOT, Mentor.
E. THOMPSON, Mesopotamia.	J. QUIGGLE, Hambden,
E. HODGES, Concord,	C. FOOT, Thompson.

MUSIC--Messrs. West, Elliott & Utley.

☞ Tickets $2.00—to be had at the bar.

Cleaveland, Sept. 1, 1818.

*Connubio jungam stabili —*VIRG.

The following letters, we lay before our readers, just as we received them--- without any other alteration than the spelling and punctuation. Several others of a similar nature have been received, but from different causes we decline presenting them to our readers.

MR, LOGAN—

I AM a young woman crossed in love. My story is very long and melancholy. I shall give you the heads of it: A young man, after having made his ap-applications to me for six months together, and filling my head with a thousand dreams of happiness, some time since, abandoned me, and is now in pursuit of another. Pray tell me in what part of the world that promontory lies, which is called the Lover's Leap, and whether one may go to it by land? But, alas, I am afraid it has lost its virtue, and that a waman of our times would find no more relief in taking such a leap, than in singing a hymn to Venus. So that I must cry out with Dido, in Dryden's Virgil, "Ah! cruel heaven, that made no cure for love!"

Your disconsolate friend.

CRÆUSA.

I shall at some future day give my fair reader a bref history of the Lover's Leap.   *Ed.*

Mr. Printer—I am a certain young woman, and love a certain young man very heartily ; and my father and mother were for it a great while, but now they say I can do better, but I think I cannot. They bid me not love him, and I cannot unlove him It is queer how they altered their opinions so soon. He is a clever fellow, and I think him pretty—I will love him for all my mother tells me not. —The man she wants me to love is a very decent looking old gentleman, and they say he is rich—and as wealth ingrosses the attention of my parents, I fear they will compel me to marry, and live wretched with a man I never can love— unless you give them a hint in your paper, to cease tormenting me about grand-pa.

Your humble servant,

K. W.

OPPOSITE: TOP LEFT

One of the very earliest recreations (later an industry) in the Western Reserve, especially in the Burton and Chardon areas where maples were abundant, was that of making maple sugar, an art brought from New England by the pioneers. The spiles driven into the sugar maples and the sap buckets were usually made of wood. A big iron kettle over an outdoor fire attracted entire families to help with the stirring and tasting of the delectable sweet.

OPPOSITE: TOP RIGHT

One of the finest examples of glacial carvings in America may be found on Kelley's Island in Lake Erie. It has been a mecca for visitors for many generations. The early settlers gazed at it with wonder and awe. Later, scientists and geologists came to observe and study this unusual formation.

OPPOSITE: BOTTOM LEFT

Invitations to the Independence Ball in Chardon in 1850 were extended to all the surrounding townships. Anyone who could spare two dollars was welcome. This party had thirty-five managers.

OPPOSITE: BOTTOM RIGHT

A favorite pastime was reading the Lovelorn column appearing in *The Cleaveland Register* in 1818. (At this time Cleaveland was still spelled with an "a.")

TOP RIGHT

The Blue Hole in Castalia is one of nature's strange phenomena. It not only attracted the Indians and the early settlers, but subsequent millions who have come to the area to marvel at its mysterious depth and blue color.

MIDDLE RIGHT

The circus, usually an annual event, caused anticipation and excitement among old and young alike. As early as 1833 Cleveland had a circus with a fire eater and Siamese twins as the main attraction. In 1842 the circus featured a camel, leopard, and giraffe as the only living specimens in the United States. The idol of the Ashtabula area was the trick horse known as Sir Henry. His owner, Edward Hamilton of Orwell, had a statue placed over his grave. It stands on Route 322 about a mile west of Windsor.

BOTTOM RIGHT

In 1838 Elizabeth Merry of Milan was invited to a select Christmas Eve dancing party at the Eagle Tavern. There were five managers for this party.

81

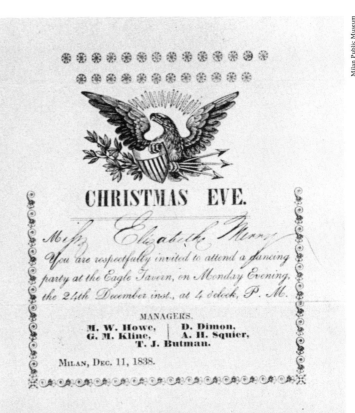

BOTTOM

Lovers' Walk on the banks of the Yellow Creek was a favorite scenic spot for picnics and leisurely walks from the time in 1803 when Turhand Kirtland brought his family to Poland, Mahoning County, until the turn of the century. Two of his grandsons, Henry Morse and C. Fitch Kirtland, are in this picture. Turhand, an agent for the Connecticut Land Company, was the father of the noted Jared Potter Kirtland.

OPPOSITE: TOP LEFT

Charles Farrar Brown joined the *Cleveland Plain Dealer* in October, 1857, as commercial editor, but in three short years won the reputation of "humorist extraordinary" because of his invention of Artemus Ward, an illiterate showman of Pittsburgh always on his way to Cleveland with his snakes, foxes, bears, and wax works. His queer spelling, his verbal quips, and his humor, used as cover for political satire, attracted a wide reading public, who became devoted to Brown and his column. He left the *Plain Dealer* to become editor of *Vanity Fair* and to give his humorous lectures in all parts of this country and even in England where he was known through his contributions to *Punch*. However, his career, which looked so promising, was cut short by tuberculosis. He died on March 6, 1867, just short of his 33rd birthday.

OPPOSITE: TOP RIGHT

Jenny Lind (1820–1887), famous Swedish singer, created a sensation when she arrived at the Weddell House in Cleveland on November 6, 1851, with a troupe of fourteen people, sponsored by the famous P. T. Barnum. Next evening she sang to a capacity audience in Kelley's Hall on the south side of Superior. Among her songs that called for encores were *Echo Song, My Jo,* and *Gypsy Song.* It was during the singing of the lovely *Bird Song* that a few nonpaying spectators crashed through the skylight, giving the audience much to talk about for many days.

OPPOSITE: BOTTOM LEFT

The Academy of Music, Cleveland, was not, as its name implies, a school for training musicians, but was a theater for the performance of dramatic productions. It was officially opened on April 16, 1853, on the top floor of a new three-story brick building on Bank Street under the name of the Cleveland Theater. The curtain went up on *The School for Scandal* played by a stock company which soon ran into financial difficulty. John A. Ellsler, well-known actor and manager, leased the theater and renamed it the Academy of Music, but instead of opening a music school he organized a stock company and dramatic school. Many future great actors had their early training here. Not until after 1860 did the Academy flourish with a variety of entertainment such as musicals, opera, drama, vaudeville, literary talks, and even a prize-fighting demonstration.

OPPOSITE: BOTTOM RIGHT

It is not surprising to find a Young Ladies Literary Society at Oberlin College, the first school to admit women to education on the college level. This Sixteenth Anniversary program (August 20, 1851) is typical of the period —lengthy dissertations interspersed with music.

JENNY LIND.

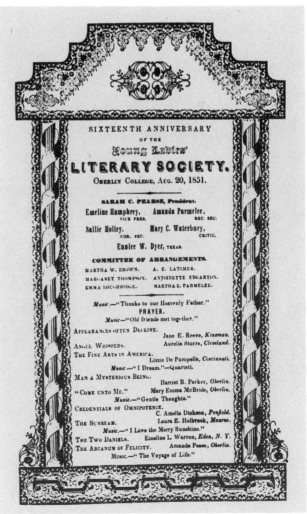

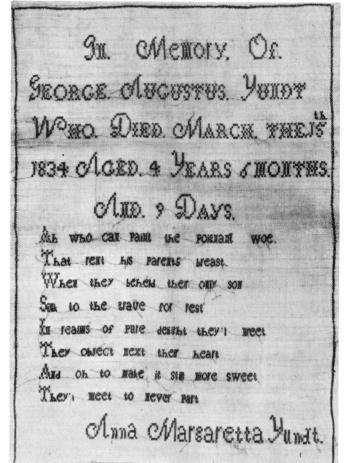

SAMPLERS

In the early 1800's samplers were the tasks of practically every little girl from the time she was able to guide a needle. The sampler served many purposes. It taught industry and perseverance, combined art and religion as well as the alphabet and numbers. Each is done in cross-stitch on hand-woven linen.

TOP LEFT

Sampler by Caroline Sarah Dunham, age 10, 1835. On display at Dunham Tavern, Cleveland.

TOP RIGHT

Sampler by Anna Margaretta Yundt, age 10, in memory of her brother, George Augustus.

Ah who can paint the poignant woe
That rent his parents breast
When they beheld their only son
Sink to the grave for rest
In realms of pure delight they'l meet
Their object next their heart
And oh to make it still more sweet
They'l meet to never part

LEFT

This double weave coverlet is two separate fabrics interwoven at the point of design. It was made by Martha Randel of Chardon in 1848.

84

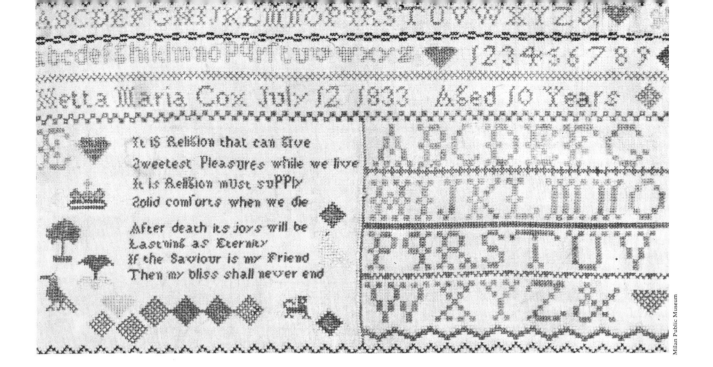

ABOVE

Sampler by Metta Maria Cox, age 10, July 12, 1833. On display at the Milan Public Museum, Milan.

It is Religion that can give
Sweetest Pleasures while we live
It is Religion must supply
Solid comforts when we die
After death its joys will be

Lasting as Eternity
If the Saviour is my Friend
Then my bliss shall never end.

BELOW

An unusually neat sampler, indicating a more mature person, was made by Lucinda A. Hatch, age 16, of Granger, Medina County, and completed on July 27, 1839.

OPPOSITE

This is not a fraktur, but a stencil, recording the birth of another child, John, in Austin Township, 1845, to the same parents as Mari Anna, indicated in her birth certificate (above). However, this certificate, made sixteen years later, is in English instead of the usual German. Birth certificate stencils, done in the manner of the Pennsylvania Dutch frakturs, are rare finds in the Western Reserve. This one is most colorful. The angels have gowns of yellow, their wings are pink and blue, and the leaves are greenish blue.

ABOVE

This fraktur tells of the birth of Mari Anna in 1829 to parents Johannes Krumm and his wife Catarina Fenstermacher of Austin Township, Trumbull County. Frakturs were country folk art of the Pennsylvania Dutch, carried into Ohio by the early settlers.

RIGHT

Often the only near likeness of the early pioneers was preserved in the silhouette, a favorite form of the arts at a time when painting supplies were difficult to obtain. This is the only picture of Henry Mason Boardman, one of the first settlers in Boardman, Mahoning County, who came to the Reserve with his bride in the Spring of 1819.

87

Lake County Historical Society

Lake County Historical Society

ABOVE

This recently discovered oil painting by an unknown artist shows the second bridge at the foot of Main Street hill in Painesville, Lake County. The bridge was built before 1819.

LEFT

Harriet Wolcott, wife of James Beard, settled in Painesville in 1823. Losing her husband the following year, she somehow managed to rear and educate her five children, two of whom became famous artists, William Holbrook Beard and James Henry Beard. This painting of her was made by one of her sons, probably William, who also made the painting of the Briggs sisters (opposite).

OPPOSITE

This primitive of Nettie and Mary Briggs of Painesville was painted in the 1840's by William Holbrook Beard, a neighbor of the Briggs family in the early years of his painting career. He and his brother James later gained fame as artists and were both elected to the National Academy of Art. The original painting has been restored and is part of an early American display in Stouffer's Cleveland restaurant on the Public Square.

The girls' father, Joseph W. Briggs, also won fame as the originator of free delivery and collection of mail in Cleveland and was appointed a special agent to establish the same service throughout the country. A tablet in his honor has been placed in the old Federal Building not very far from the restaurant where the primitive painting of his daughters is hung.

89

ABOVE

An unknown artist's sketch shows Main Street, Wellington, Lorain County, as it appeared in 1857. The second building to the left of the church was the old American House, founded in 1833 as the Wadsworth Inn.

LEFT

A popular pastime in the 1850's and for several decades later was making wreaths suitable for framing. Women collected hair of various shades or yarn of different hues and wove them into intricate floral patterns. This one made of feathers is quite unusual. It was made in Milan, Erie County, by an unknown artist.

BELOW

Norman Hall, Sandusky, a three-story stone structure, was built near the northeast corner of Water and Decatur Streets, to answer the need for headquarters and a place to display art works for the newly organized Cosmopolitan Art and Literary Association. At the second Annual Drawing on February 28, 1856, a brilliant throng of over a thousand persons from all over the country gathered to witness the distribution of art treasures.

Sandusky became a center of the Arts from 1854 to 1860 during the time it was headquarters for the Cosmopolitan Art and Literary Association, a national organization. Membership was made up of individuals who had purchased through the Art Association, for three dollars, a subscription to one of the popular magazines of the day, such as *Harper's, Putnam's,* and *Godey's.* Profit was used to buy works of art. With each subscription went one ticket for the drawing to be held annually. At the end of the first year, membership from all over the country had reached 22,418. At that time 160 works of art were distributed, among them Hiram Powers' famous statue of a Greek Slave, valued at $5,000. The organization grew and members received increased benefits, including a monthly bulletin devoted to the advancement of art and literature. These pictures were taken from the Second Annual Catalogue, 1855–1856.

RIGHT
Notice of organization.

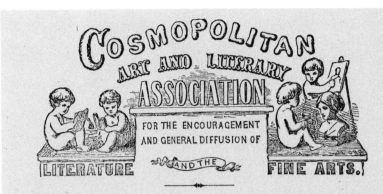

THIS new Art Association, organized June, 1854, is designed to encourage and popularize the Fine Arts, and disseminate wholesome Literature throughout the country.

A Gallery of Art has been permanently founded, and will contain annually a choice and valuable collection of Paintings, Statuary, &c., which are to be allotted to members at the annual distribution of each year. The best Literature of the day will be issued to Subscribers, consisting of the various Monthly Magazines.

Both Cosmopolitan Art Journal

91

LEFT

This rooster weathervane was carved from poplar wood and painted red. Made about 1860, it came from the Miller barn in Havana, Huron County.

BELOW

Among the earliest settlers in Twinsburg, Summit County, were twin brothers, Aaron and Moses Wilcox, merchants from Connecticut who had married sisters and then decided to settle in the Reserve. To the little town of Millsville they offered land for a public square and $20 toward erection of a school, if the name were changed to Twinsburg. This primitive painting was done by an unknown artist.

92

Politics

In the political arena during the half century before the Civil War, the Reserve produced many outstanding statesmen, witnessed a major naval battle of the War of 1812, and became a hotbed of abolitionism.

The Western Reserve gave the state of Ohio three governors before 1860. Samuel Huntington was elected from Trumbull County in 1808, Seabury Ford from Geauga County in 1848, and Reuben Wood from Cuyahoga County in 1850.

LEFT

Samuel Huntington (1767–1817), Western Reserve's first governor of Ohio, nephew and namesake of Governor Huntington of Connecticut, has been described as "a man of wealth and culture, small in stature with an affable manner, who readily won the confidence of the populace." Coming to Ohio in 1800 to explore the area, he liked what he saw and the following year returned with his wife, his two sons, and their governess. He intended to settle in Youngstown, but soon changed his mind and built a pretentious log house in Cleveland on the bluff south of Superior. Among his land purchases was sublot 84 for which he paid $1.12 (site of Higbee's). Like other early Yale graduates and lawyers, he entered the political field and held many offices including state senator from Trumbull County, judge of the Supreme Court, delegate to the convention to form a State Constitution, and finally governor of Ohio (1808–1810). In 1813 he and General William Henry Harrison came to Cleveland to establish a fort at the foot of Seneca facing the lake, known as Fort Huntington in his honor. At the end of his service as paymaster in the War of 1812, he retired to his farm in Painesville.

CENTER

Seabury Ford (1801–1855), the Western Reserve's second governor of Ohio, came to Burton from New Haven with his parents when he was six years old. His early education was secured at the Burton Academy. When he and a friend were ready for college they decided it must be Yale, but because of lack of funds they made the entire journey on foot. After graduation in 1825 he returned to Burton, studied law with his uncle Peter Hitchcock, was admitted to the bar, married, served in the State Militia, and joined the newly organized Whig party. He was elected to the Ohio Legislature many times, was chosen Speaker of the House in the 39th Assembly and Speaker of the Senate in the 44th. He became an expert on tax and banking legislation. His most notable achievement was securing the repeal of the Loan Law in 1837, which permitted the State of Ohio to loan money to the railroads. During his administration as governor (1848–1850), the Black Laws, which discriminated against the negro, were repealed. He was the last Whig governor of Ohio.

RIGHT

Reuben Wood (1792–1864) was the third Western Reserve settler to serve as governor of Ohio. This tall Vermonter with the powerful frame, pleasing disposition, and ready wit, was welcomed to the small community of Cleveland in 1818, becoming president of the village three years later. An excellent lawyer and fluent speaker, he was called upon to deliver addresses on many occasions, two of the most important being the opening of the Ohio Canal in 1827 and the first run of the Cleveland, Columbus, and Cincinnati Railroad in 1851. He was elected to the State Senate for three terms and the Supreme Court for two terms, one as Chief Justice. He served as governor of Ohio from December, 1850, to July, 1853, when he resigned to accept the diplomatic appointment as consulate at Valparaiso, Chile. In 1854 he retired to his home, Evergreen Place, on Lake Erie in the vicinity of Avalon and Wagar Road in Rocky River.

93

WAR!

A way letter from a gentleman at the city of Washington, to his friend in Philadelphia, dated on Tuesday last says "The WAR BILL has just passed the Senate 19 to 13."

June 19, 1812.

[*Lanc. Journal.*

PITTSBURGH, *June 25, 1812.*

Extract of a letter from Mr. Lacock to a gentleman in this Town, dated Washington City, June 18 1812.

"I embrace the first opportunity to inform you that *WAR* has this day been declared, and the injunction of secrecy taken off. This measure passed in the House of Representatives by a majority of 30, and in Senate 19 to 13. This is an unqualified, unconditional War, by land and sea, against the United Kingdoms of Great Britain and Ireland."

LEFT

The *Trump of Fame* at Warren, first newspaper in the Western Reserve, published news of war on July 1, 1812, thirteen days after war had been declared against Great Britain. It is not reported as a dispatch from the government, but in the form of a letter from Washington to a friend in Philadelphia.

BELOW

O'Mic (or Omique), the Indian, was hung on the gallows on Cleveland's Public Square, June 24, 1812. News reached Warren in time for the July first publication of *Trump of Fame.*

OPPOSITE: LEFT

An editorial in the *Trump of Fame* predicts war with France and comments on some of the reasons of this second war with Great Britain.

OPPOSITE: TOP RIGHT

An added inducement to enlist for a term of five years during the War of 1812 was the promise of bounty of $16, three months pay, and 160 acres of land.

OPPOSITE: BOTTOM RIGHT

One of the Reserve's earliest political figures was John Walworth (1765–1812), purchaser of 2,000 acres in Painesville Township, where he brought his family in the winter of 1800 after a trip over the ice along Lake Erie. Shortly after his home was erected he was called upon to serve the community in various capacities. He was appointed a justice of the peace for Trumbull County in 1802, an associate judge in 1803, postmaster of Painesville in 1804. During 1806 he held three jobs of importance, collector of the district of Erie, associate judge of Geauga County, and postmaster of Cleveland where he established a residence and became active in local politics. When Cuyahoga County was organized he was elected county clerk and recorder, an office he held until his death in 1812.

By a gentleman just from Cleveland, we are informed, that Omique the Indian, who was under sentence of death for the murder of two men committed on Pipe creek, Huron county, was executed at Cleveland on Friday last. We are informed, that there were no Indians present at the execution. Four companies of militia performed the duties of a military escort, on this occasion.

TRUMP of FAME.
WEDNESDAY......JULY 1.

We have given in our paper, this week, an extract from one of the letters composing the correspondence, between the Secretary of State and our minister at the court of France. Our readers will learn, from this, some of the grounds of complaint, which our country has against France,

The size of a country paper will hardly permit the insertion of so lengthy a correspondence. Perhaps, at some future time we may give a general summary of it.

We announce to our patrons, this week, the all important news of a declaration of WAR, by the United States, against the United Kingdoms of Great Britain and Ireland. Brought by the orders in council again into a state of colonial vassalage, the United States, after almost the completion of thirty six years, have been obliged again to arise in the majesty of their might, and to declare that "these States are and of right ought to be free and independent"

This great event will call to recollection the eventful period of '76—"the time, which tried mens souls. None but those who then were in active life, can realize the circumstances of those times. The historic page, but dimly, reflects upon most of the present generation a knowledge of those times of distress. To run a parrallel between the resources of these States, at that time and the present, is extremely gratifying to our pride. It must be highly painful to a mind of sensibility, to know the degree of patriotism, that burnt in the bosoms of the heroes of that day, and observe the lukewarmness of the present race. On the fourth day of this ever memorable month, the embargo, with which we have been for some time past shackled, expires and thirty six years will be completed, between the first and second declaration of independence.

From a review of the whole correspondence, between Mr. Barlow and the French minister, the Duke Bassano, it will not be, perhaps, too presumptuous in the editor of a country news.paper to say, that our government will declare war against France, before the expiration of the year, unless she should adopt a different system of measures towards the United States.

TO MEN OF PATRIOT-ISM, COURAGE AND ENTERPRIZE.

EVERY able bodied man, from the age of 18 to 45 years, who shall be enlisted for the term of five years, will be paid a bounty of SIXTEEN DOLLARS—and whenever he shall have served the term for which he enlisted, and obtained an honorable discharge, stating that he had faithfully performed his duty whilst in service, he shall be allowed and paid, in addition to the aforesaid bounty, *three months pay, and* ONE HUNDRED *and* SIXTY ACRES OF LAND ; and in case he should be killed in action or die in the service, his heirs and representatives will be entitled to the said three months' pay, and one hundred and sixty acres of land, to be designated, surveyed and laid off, at the public expence.

WILSON ELLIOTT,
Capt. U. States' Army.

Warren, July 6th, 1812.

Place of Rendezvous, Warren, Trumbull Co. Ohio.

For 150 years Oliver Hazard Perry (1785–1819) and his notable deeds have captured the imagination of youthful Americans. His military career began at the age of fourteen when he left his home in Rhode Island to become a midshipman on a vessel bound for the West Indies in search of pirates. When the War of 1812 broke out, he was put in command of a flotilla of gunboats and later ordered to equip boats for military service on Lake Erie. Most of the boats were built in Erie, Pennsylvania, but three were constructed on the Cuyahoga River (near Akron). For excitement and glamor Perry's career was an enviable one. For daring bravado his capture of the British fleet seems almost unreal. Even after his spectacular victory in the Battle of Lake Erie, his search for adventure carried him to the Mediterranean and the West Indies. Here he fell victim to yellow fever and died at age 34, bringing to a close a life filled with peril and excitement.

BELOW

Young, handsome, impulsive Commodore Oliver Hazard Perry fired his men with his own enthusiasm during the Battle of Lake Erie, September 10, 1813. When his flagship Lawrence was almost completely wrecked, the Commodore escaped in a small boat amid a shower of cannon and musket balls. Reaching one of his nine vessels, the Niagara, which was undamaged, he hoisted the flag of the Lawrence with its famous emblem "Don't give up the ship!" and relentlessly pursued the British until they could hold out no longer. His victory astounded both sides and turned the tide of the war in favor of the United States. His message to General William Henry Harrison, commander-in-chief of the northwestern army, reflects his pride and exuberance. "We have met the enemy and they are ours, two ships, two brigs, one schooner, and one sloop."

A. Lawson after painting by Gilbert Stuart, W.R.H.S.

A. Lawson after painting by Thomas Birch, W.R.H.S.

Slayton Underhill for *Time,* July 1944, W.R.H.S.

ABOVE

This animated and vibrant picture is an artist's conception of the unsuccessful British attempt to land in Cleveland during the War of 1812. It creates the impression of a few villagers rushing to the defence of the small settlement. In reality Cleveland was considered a strategic point and for a few months there were more soldiers than settlers. Local militia companies from Cleveland, Doans Corners, and Newburg patrolled the lake. They were augmented by Major Jessup's regulars and a force from Major General Elijah Wadsworth's army stationed at Old Portage ready for action. In May, 1813, Captain Stanton Sholes and his company from Beavertown, Pennsylvania, arrived with orders to aid in the defence of Cleveland. He built a hospital and a fort and was an eye witness to the attempted landing. Said Captain Sholes: "On the 19th of June, 1813, a part of the British fleet appeared off our harbor with the apparent design to land. When they got within one and a half miles it became perfectly calm and they lay there till after noon when a most terrible thunder storm came up and drove them from our coast. We saw them no more as enemies."

RIGHT

A year before Perry's great victory, volunteer troops marched from Portage County to the Sandusky area to defend the Reserve from British attack. This notice in the July 1, 1812, issue of *Trump of Fame,* glorifies Ohio's patriotic spirit.

We are informed, that the volunteer corps raised within the limits of Col. John Campbell's regiment, Portage county, have received orders, from Governor Meigs to march to Sandusky to protect the United States store at that place and guard that part of our frontier; and that they will march to-morrow from Ravenna.

Much praise is due to this regiment for their readiness to obey their countries call. We believe, that even in the patriotic state of Ohio; and she is second to none in the Union; very few regiments alone have furnished a complete company of volunteers. Officers and men, without claim, or regard to rank, volunteered as privates. Col Campbell, in common with the private centinel, shouldered his rifle, and took a common lot for a command in the corps. He has been honored by the unanimous suffrage of his fellow soldiers with the captaincy of the company.

97

TOP LEFT

This courthouse, built in 1806 of hewn black walnut logs by Abraham Skinner of New Market, Painesville Township, served all of Geauga County which at that time embraced the present Geauga, Ashtabula, Cuyahoga, and Lake counties. It stood at the junction of North State Street and Skinner Avenue.

BOTTOM LEFT

The Brecksville Museum, built in 1835 by Charles Rich, is still called the Squire Rich House. As Justice of the Peace for thirty years he heard suits in his home, often referred to as the courthouse. A simple country home, it has been partially furnished as a primitive dwelling by the Brecksville Historical Society. Displays in most of the rooms include relics of the early settlement.

BELOW

This Town Hall, situated on the green opposite the Congregational Church in Tallmadge, was built by public subscription in 1859. An academy occupied the second floor providing instruction in both high school and college subjects for students from many communities. Design of the facade is Greek revival with four Doric pilasters supporting a plain pediment.

Henry Howe

Henry Howe

Early Homes of Ohio by I. T. Frary

ABOVE LEFT

Benjamin F. Wade (1800–1878), a self-made man, who never attended school, became an avid reader under his mother's tutelage and at eighteen was better informed than most of his companions. Like Giddings he secured his legal training in the office of Elisha Whittlesey and then formed a partnership with Giddings in the town of Jefferson. A large-framed man, six feet tall, an original thinker and forthright speaker, he attracted willing listeners to the cause of abolition, but his ready wit at the expense of his opponents made him many enemies. Elected to the United States Senate, he served from 1852 to 1870 as one of our most vigorous defenders of human rights. He was elected President of the Senate and in that capacity automatically became acting vice president under Andrew Johnson. Had one more senator voted for impeachment of Johnson, Wade would have become President of the United States.

ABOVE RIGHT

Joshua Reed Giddlings (1795–1864), a veteran of the War of 1812 and a school teacher turned lawyer, started his legal practice in Jefferson where he won the admiration and respect of the townspeople. Elected to Congress in 1838 as a Whig, he opposed for the next twenty years every measure which favored slavery. A large man of great physical strength and commanding delivery, he struck fear into many of his opponents. In 1842 he defied the Atherton Gag Rule prohibiting discussion of slavery on the House floor. Censured by the House, he resigned, but a few weeks later was re-elected by an overwhelming majority. He continued his defiance and thereby restored constitutional freedom of speech in our Congress. In 1856 he wrote the draft of the first Republican platform. In 1858 he was appointed U. S. Consul to Canada where he spent the rest of his life.

BELOW

The famous Jefferson law office, still standing, was built by Joshua Reed Giddings in 1823. He formed a partnership with Benjamin F. Wade, another staunch abolitionist, from 1831–1835 when they shared this small building consisting of an office and consultation room. Furnishings were simple: a few chairs, a large table, shelves for law books, a high desk, a box stove for wood, and a sheet-iron safe—the first brought to Ashtabula County.

TOP LEFT

Elisha Whittlesey (1783–1863) was one of the most prominent figures of the early Western Reserve. At age 24 he came from Milford, Connecticut, with his young wife Polly Mygatt to settle in Canfield, where they built a home and raised ten children. To Elisha is due the legal training of many brilliant lawyers of his day, Wade and Giddings among them. He served Trumbull County as prosecuting attorney, was elected to several terms in the Ohio Legislature and in 1823 was elected to Congress where he represented the district until 1838. President Harrison appointed him auditor of the Post Office Department in 1841 and then later first Comptroller of the U. S. Treasury. He continued to hold the latter office during the administrations of Presidents Taylor, Fillmore, and Pierce, resigning during Buchanan's term but serving again under Lincoln. This is a little seen photoengraving of him as a young man.

TOP RIGHT

Betsey Cowles, youngest daughter of the Rev. Giles Hooker Cowles, who came to Austinburg as the Congregational minister in 1811, was a prime example of an independent woman, so rare in the early days of the Reserve. A graduate of Oberlin in the third class, she entered the teaching field, serving select schools in Portsmouth, Canton, Massillon, and Painesville, and for several years took charge of the Grand River Institute as principal of the female department. She has been credited with introducing kindergarten classes.

Shocked by the treatment of runaway slaves, she became a staunch advocate of the anti-slavery movement, making forceful speeches which won many supporters to the cause. Because of rebuffs she received due to her sex, she championed "Women's Rights" and was chosen to preside at the National Suffrage Convention in 1850. Edwin Cowles, editor of the Cleveland *Leader,* was her nephew. He, too, became a supporter of the anti-slavery movement and of the Republican party.

SLAVERY AND THE UNDERGROUND

Nowhere in Ohio was the anti-slavery movement more rampant than in the Western Reserve. It was the shelter of many an Underground Railroad station through which numerous slaves were spirited away to freedom. As early as 1837 negro fugitives sought Oberlin as a haven and means of escape. They were supported by the poor funds, and charges for food and lodging were recorded in the township records. However, complications arose when Congress passed the Fugitive Slave Law in 1850, making it mandatory for federal agents to assist southern slave hunters in tracking down slaves escaping to the north. Any person caught interfering might be subject to a fine of $1,000 and imprisonment for six months. In 1858 this law was put to the test in Oberlin, when John Price, an escaped slave, had been forceably taken to Wellington by three men who intended to return him to his master. Word spread quickly in Oberlin and there was a mass exodus of students and professors to Wellington where they rescued Price and eventually succeeded in getting him to Canada and freedom.

All the suspected participants were arrested. Those from Wellington were given nominal fines and allowed to go home. Most from Oberlin were given the same privilege but they chose to stay in Cuyahoga County jail where they could arouse sympathy of the populace and discredit the Fugitive Slave Law. Sheriff David Long Wightman and Jailer Smith, both staunch Republicans, did all they could to make their prisoners comfortable. A shoemaking

The Oberlin Rescuers.
At Cuyahoga Co. jail April 1859.

1 2 3 4 5 6 7 8 9 10 11 12 13 14 15 16 17 18 19 20

1 J. R. Shepard.   5 W. Evans.   9 S. Bushnell.   13 A. W. Lyman.   17 J. Watson.
2 O. S. B. Wall.   6 E. Boyce.   10 J. Scott.   14 J. Bartlett.   18 J. M. Fitch.
3 L. Wadsworth.   7 R. Plumb.   11 M. Gillett.   15 W. E. Lincoln.   19 H. E. Peck.
4 D. Watson.   8 H. Evans.   12 C. Langston.   16 R. Winsor.   20 D. Williams.

Harold Brandt

Mrs. Robert Fletcher

shop was installed in one cell, harness making in another, cabinetmaking in a third. They even set up a newspaper and managed to get out one issue of *The Rescuer,* July 4, 1859, two days before all prisoners were released. They were escorted to the train by a guard of honor of Cleveland citizens and were welcomed by a record crowd, the mayor, and a brass band when they arrived in Oberlin.

This intense opposition against the Fugitive Slave Law brought about the rise of the Republican party, greater respect for Oberlin, and paved the way for whole-hearted support of the Civil War.

ABOVE
The Rescuers in front of the Cuyahoga County jail include Oberlin students, a negro shoemaker, an attorney, a professor, a Sunday school superintendent, and a book store proprietor.

RIGHT
The drawing made by Oberlin Professor Charles H. Churchill in 1858 shows students decoying "man stealers" into the woods at the right while fugitive slaves escape to the left.

101

RIGHT
Henry Everard Peck, associate professor of intellectual and moral philosophy, was among those imprisoned for his alleged part in the rescue. While in jail he was permitted to preach from the doorway to the crowd gathered in the Cleveland jail yard.

BELOW
Bulletins like this were posted all over Oberlin calling for a public meeting to welcome the Rescuers, just released from jail, July 6, 1859.

OUT OF JAIL!
THE RESCUERS
Are coming TO-NIGHT !

At a public Meeting at the Mayor's Office it was voted that the citizens, en masse, turn out to meet them at the CARS, and escort them to the Church for Public Reception. The undersigned were appointed a Committee of Arrangements:

H. L. HENRY,   A. N. BEECHER,   W. P. HARRIS.
J. M. ELLIS,   E. R. STILES.

The committee appointed Father Keep for President of the Meeting at the church, and Prof. J. M. Ellis, Marshall. All the citizens are invited to meet the Rescuers at the Depot at half-past seven. The procession will form after the Band in the following order:

The Mayor and Council; The Fire Department in Uniform; The Rescuers; The Citizens.

Let there be a grand gathering !
Oberlin, July 6.   By order of Committee of Arrangements.

Roads and Taverns

Without adequate transportation, isolated communities changed very slowly. But with the construction of plank roads, better coaches and more luxurious accommodations, travel among the towns of the Reserve became more common, bringing gradual changes. The need to transport agricultural products to market, to visit friends in other communities, and to carry on business transactions encouraged the building of plank roads. Although the planks rotted quickly, they did serve as invaluable all-weather surfaces while they lasted. Without some kind of paving, roads turned into impassable mud-holes with every heavy rain. The first scheduled overland transportation was the mail coach, which often accommodated passengers. As early as 1837, the Cleveland Directory advertised passenger stagecoach travel between Cleveland and Pittsburgh. Many other routes connected all the major towns in the Western Reserve. Jolly drivers, such as Josh Jocks on the Cleveland-Warren route, entertained passengers with their news and gossip of the day, bringing relief from the monotony and discomfort of tedious journeys.

This increase in highway travel brought a demand for taverns which vied with each other in offering the best accommodations. Cleveland's Franklin House won renown for its cleanliness and good food, a rare combination. Often a tavern was the first two or three-story building in a community, built by a master craftsman who embellished the design with classical columns and detailing. Visiting celebrities received the best rooms and dined in the large banquet halls where townspeople gathered to hear their speeches.

Although roads, coaches, and taverns brought an increase of activity, they were still a part of the simple, unhurried rural and small-town life that characterized the Western Reserve until the coming of the railroads in the 'fifties.

The Rockport Plank Road Company was incorporated in 1848. Planks were laid on Detroit Road from West 25th Street in Cleveland to five miles beyond Rocky River, including a bridge across the river. This road was a boon to produce farmers who could now bring their crops into Cleveland where a ready market awaited them. Toll gates were established at regular intervals to help pay for the road. Charges were moderate as may be seen from this toll chart which hung at the toll gate house at Warren and Detroit until 1901.

Western Reserve Historical Society

RATES OF TOLL.

For Every Wagon, Cart, Carriage or Buggy Drawn by 1 Horse		5¢
" " " " " Drawn by 2 Horses or Oxen		10 "
" " Horse in Addition		3 "
" " Sled or Sleigh drawn by 1 Horse		4 "
" " " " " " 2 Horses		6 "
" " Horse in Addition		3 "
" " Horse and Rider		4 "
" " Horse, Mule or Ass Led or Driven		1 "
" " Head of Neat Cattle		⅓ "
" " " " Sheep or Hogs		⅙ "
" " Stage Coach, Hack or Omnibus		
" " Drawn by 2 Horses		12 "
" " Horse in Addition		3 "
" " Bicycle, Tricycle or Velocipede		4 "

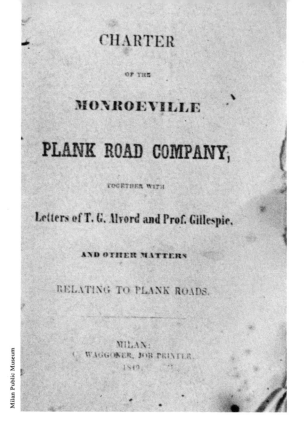

LEFT

The 1840's witnessed the building of plank roads in many communities to answer a crying need for better transportation. As soon as plank road companies were incorporated, gangs of workmen proceeded to lay firm beds of logs, covering them with two-inch planks. A charter was granted in 1849 to the Monroeville Plank Road Company, Huron County, a copy of which is now on exhibit at the Milan Historical Museum.

BELOW

By 1849 Cleveland was planked in many directions, with roads leading to Chagrin Falls, Willoughby, Twinsburg, Wooster, and Rockport. A section of Lorain Street was also ready. This is the toll house and gate at Lorain and West 65th Street. A wagon with one horse, regardless of the load, was charged five cents, which is probably all this milk driver paid. Grandma sits in the sun and watches the plank-road traffic clatter by.

RIGHT
Stagecoach schedule.

BELOW
The Old Beebe Tavern, built in Elyria, Lorain County, by pioneer Artemus Beebe in 1818, was for many years the principal hostelry in the village and the stagecoach station for the Cleveland-Fremont route.

Summer Arrangement of Mail Coaches from Elyria.

DAILY.

The Mail will leave this place, daily, for Detroit and Cleveland, as follows:—
For CLEVELAND, - at 6 o'clock, A. M.
For DETROIT, - - - at 10 o'clock, A. M.
☞ Passengers conveyed in Post Coaches

Three Times a Week.

The Mail Stage will leave Elyria—
For OBERLIN, at 1 o'clock, P. M., on TUESDAYS, THURSDAYS, and SATURDAYS.
☞ For seats, apply at the *Stage Office.* East end of Broad street.

Extras furnished on short notice, and on reasonable terms.
All baggage at the risk of the owners.
A. BEEBE, Proprietor.
Elyria, May 23, 1837.   48

105

LEFT

During the 1850's and early 1860's, the best-known driver of the stagecoach from Cleveland to Warren was Josh Jocks (Jox), a genial "Dutchman" who knew everyone along his route, delivered their mail, and was willing to dispense all the news as he heard it from other passengers. According to early notations from the diary of Jane Church of Chagrin Falls who often rode with Josh to Parkman where her father had a blacksmith shop, it took from 9:30 a.m. to 4:00 p.m. for the trip of about seventeen miles. In winter it was a long, cold ride with no heat in the coach. When Josh stopped at the Bayard Tavern in Chagrin Falls to change horses, young riders vied with each other for the privilege of sitting with him on the high front seat.

BELOW

Bayard Tavern, located on the northeast corner of Main and Orange Streets, Chagrin Falls, Cuyahoga County, was built in 1834. A couple of years later it became the stagecoach stop on the road between Cleveland and Warren. The house on the hill, the third frame dwelling built in the village, was erected by Noah Graves. The grove of trees surrounding the house gave the site the name Grove Hill.

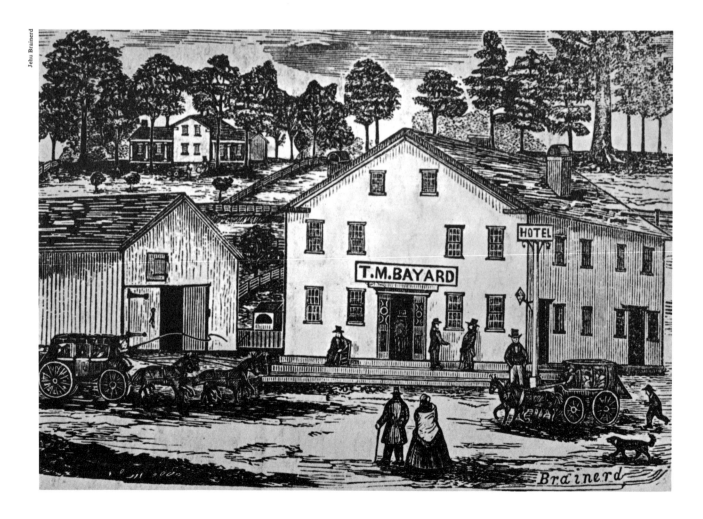

T.M. BAYARD

HOTEL

Brainerd

This advertisement appeared in the Cleveland Directory, July, 1837.

On August 11, 1818, stagecoach travel was inaugurated between Cleveland and Painesville, leaving every Thursday with an overnight stop at Chagrin. These coaches were springless wagons with plain board seats. They also carried the mail. In 1820 stages were traveling to Columbus and the following year to Pittsburgh and Buffalo. By 1847 there were five stages daily from Cleveland to Buffalo. A favorite stop was the Franklin House in Painesville, Lake County.

PIONEER FAST STAGE LINE

From CLEVELAND to PITTSBURG,

Leaves daily at 8 o'clock A. M., via *Bedford, Hudson, Ravenna, Deerfield, Salem* and *New Lisbon*, to Wellsville, where they will take the

STEAM BOATS.

Jehu Brainerd

FRANKLIN HOUSE,
(REBUILT AND IMPROVED IN 1848:)
BY SAM'L BURRIDGE, JR.,
PAINESVILLE, OHIO.

The Eastern, Western and Southern Stages, call at this House for passengers.

107

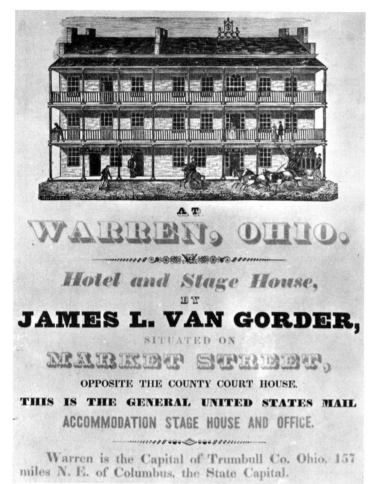

AT WARREN, OHIO.

Hotel and Stage House,

BY

JAMES L. VAN GORDER,

SITUATED ON

MARKET STREET,

OPPOSITE THE COUNTY COURT HOUSE.

THIS IS THE GENERAL UNITED STATES MAIL

ACCOMMODATION STAGE HOUSE AND OFFICE.

Warren is the Capital of Trumbull Co. Ohio, 157 miles N. E. of Columbus, the State Capital.

LEFT

This hotel and stage house in Warren, Trumbull County, was known in its early days as Castle William. After its purchase in 1828 by James L. Van Gorder, it was called the Pavilion and became a popular stop for stagecoaches. Van Gorder, a keen businessman, saw greater opportunities when the canal was built. He decided that building canal locks was more remunerative than managing a tavern. The Pavilion, which had seen many gay events and had housed thousands of travelers, fell into neglect. It burned in 1846.

BELOW

This frame building, erected about 1836 by Asael Adams, Jr., at the intersection of Market and Park Avenue in Warren, was a tavern called the Franklin House. Asael came from Canterbury, Connecticut, to the Reserve at the age of fourteen with his father and brother-in-law, Camden Cleaveland, brother of Moses Cleaveland. He had an interesting early career, as a teacher in Cleveland in 1805, and as a pony express rider during the War of 1812, carrying United States mail on horseback from Cleveland to Pittsburgh.

Harold Byland

108

BELOW

On May 14, 1824, Rufus Dunham purchased thirteen and three-fourths acres on Euclid Road, Cleveland, for $147 and proceeded to erect a log cabin which served his family (and for a time another family) until 1832 when he began construction of the frame house later known as Dunham Tavern. On the busy Buffalo-Cleveland-Detroit Highway, it was a favorite stopping place for weary travelers until 1857 when it was purchased for a summer home by a Cleveland family. In 1941 the Society of Collectors came into possession of the house and restored it as a tavern of those long ago pioneer days.

RIGHT

The fireplace is in the west wing of Dunham Tavern. The fine portrait over the mantel is by an unknown artist. The chairs, tankards, and candlesticks are authentic for the early 1800's.

LEFT

The Brecksville Inn was the oldest hotel in continuous service in Cuyahoga County until 1913 when it was remodeled by the Brecksville Country Club. The inn was built mostly of black walnut in 1839. The huge fireplace and interior were left unchanged. Theodore Breck, pioneer member of the State Senate for several terms and builder and owner of the hotel, is sitting on the porch to the left.

BELOW

This busy traffic scene of Cleveland's west Superior Street was sketched on the spot by Henry Howe in 1846. To the right is the Weddell House, a four-story sandstone and brick with octagonal cupola and pillared balcony, most famous of Cleveland's early hotels. Farther down the street can be seen the Franklin House, erected by Philo Scovill to meet the demand of stagecoach travel to Cleveland. The American House is on the south side of the street next to the Merchants Exchange. In the center, about where the High Level Bridge starts today, is Hilliard and Hayes, dry goods and grocery merchants.

OPPOSITE: TOP RIGHT

The Rider Tavern in Painesville, Lake County, is another of the impressive buildings credited to the genius of Jonathan Goldsmith. Modeled after Mt. Vernon, the six square columns are functional as well as decorative, for they actually support the roof. There is some disagreement as to the date of construction, but the general opinion is 1822.

110

MIDDLE RIGHT

The Stone Tavern in Poland, Mahoning County, was built by Jonathan Fowler in 1804. His wife Lydia was the sister of Turhand Kirtland, agent for the Connecticut Land Company. This tavern was for many years a stagecoach stop between Pittsburgh and Cleveland. It was during a stop here that Thaddeus Kosciusko, a Polish patriot and aide to General George Washington during the American Revolution, scratched with a diamond on one of the window panes:

> Old Poland neath the Northern Star
>   has yielded up the ghost;
> But Poland new the wreath shall bear;
>   the young Ohio's boast.

The town of Poland was so named by Turhand Kirtland because of his deep sympathy for the oppressed Poles, saying "Here will be a Poland that is free."

BOTTOM RIGHT

The Reid House at Black River (now Lorain) was built in 1835 by Conrad Reid, an 1811 pioneer, landlord, shipbuilder, and first mayor of the village.

BELOW

Col. John Singletary's original Stagecoach Inn, Streetsboro, Portage County, long famous for the beautiful fanlight over the doorway, was built in 1826. It was a favorite stopping place for passengers between Pittsburgh and Cleveland.

Perry Cragg

Early Homes of Ohio by I. T. Frary

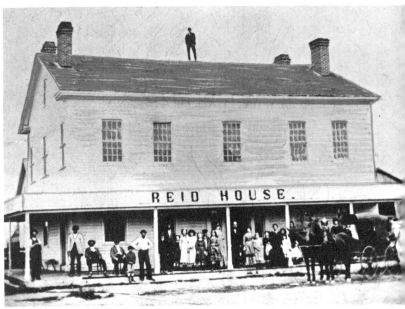

George Kirtland Bishop

111

Lorain County Historical Society

The Franklin House on Superior near Water Street, Cleveland, was built in 1826 by Philo Scovill to meet the demand of stagecoach travel. It was the first white, frame, three-story tavern in the Reserve and it soon won renown for its cleanliness and good food. At this time coaches were operating only twice a week between Cleveland and Pittsburgh. However, comfortable travel accommodations between Cleveland and Erie could be secured each day on the mail coach for only $3.00. This was a popular stopping place for all stage lines and the rendezvous for itinerant lawyers and lake captains.

OPPOSITE: BOTTOM

The American House in Wellington, Lorain County, formerly the Wadsworth Inn, was built in 1833. This hotel was the scene of the famed Oberlin-Wellington slave rescue episode in 1858. It was demolished in 1902 for construction of the Herrick Memorial Library.

RIGHT

The Forest City House came into being in 1852 on the site of the present Cleveland-Sheraton Hotel on Cleveland's Public Square. Four other hotels or taverns had preceded it from the early days of the settlement. Plinney Mowery erected his log tavern in May, 1815, on the land he had purchased from Samuel Huntington for $100 a few years before. Next came the Cleveland House in 1822. In 1832 it was razed and the three-story City Hotel took its place. Ten years later, the proprietor, James W. Cook, banned the sale of liquor and renamed it the Cleveland Temperance House. Fire destroyed it in 1845. In 1848 a new brick hotel called the Dunham House was erected. Additions were made when it became the Forest City House. It served Cleveland visitors until September 16, 1915, when it was torn down for the present hotel.

Western Reserve Historical Society

BELOW

American House, opened in 1837, was the first large hotel in Cleveland. For the next ten years it was the scene of fine balls and banquets and speeches from the balcony by presidential candidate William Henry Harrison and Ohio candidate for governor, Thomas Corwin. Popularity of the hotel waned when the new Weddell House across the street opened its doors in 1847.

PART THREE

Commercial Fever

Completion of the Erie Canal through New York state in 1825 brought some trade to the Lake Erie towns, but not until the opening of the Akron-Cleveland section of the Ohio Canal in 1827 did the Reserve have an outlet for its agricultural produce and cattle. At last the products of the Reserve could be transported cheaply and exchanged for east coast or European manufactured goods hitherto unavailable or secured at great cost. Commercial fever hit even small towns which needed a larger market than the local neighborhood. Canal boats met lake freighters and transferred their loads of grain, cattle, lumber, barrel staves, and whiskey to be carried to far-off ports.

The discovery of iron and copper deposits around Lake Superior opened the way for Cleveland to become a great manufacturing and commercial center. By 1854 thousands of tons of ore were being shipped by freighters to the Reserve, portending a boom in iron and steel for the next century. The coming of the railroads in the 1850's stepped up commercial activity and rendered the canals passé. With the faster rail transportation, perishable goods could be safely shipped, thus opening a wider market and bringing more prosperity to the Reserve. As industry developed, activity centered around ship building, iron and steel manufacturing, and coal mining.

An important link in the development of industry was the stabilization of Ohio's banking system. Three men who helped to get finances on a sound footing were Alfred Kelley, Truman Handy, and General Simon Perkins.

A view of Cleveland in 1853 (from the hill west of the river) shows the warehouse and commission establishments along the Cuyahoga River. The broad street in the center is Superior with Euclid Avenue angling off to the right.

Canals

TOP LEFT
This sketch of the canal boy from the Horatio Alger series is said to represent James A. Garfield at the time he drove a canal boat from the coal mines of Governor Tod at Brier Hill to Cleveland during the summer of 1848. In 1857 Garfield became president of Hiram College and in 1859 was elected to the Ohio Senate. He became President of the United States in 1881 but was assassinated a few months after he took office.

BOTTOM LEFT
One of the most versatile and dynamic men to mold Cleveland and Ohio in its early days was Alfred Kelley (1789–1859), first president of the Village of Cleveland and of its earliest bank. Due to his clear thinking, exceptional foresight, and tenacious persistence, the entire area west of the Alleghenies grew in population and prosperity. The Ohio Canal, for which he was mainly responsible, opened trade as nothing else could have done; the banking reconstruction under his guidance brought financial stability; his promotion of the railroads stimulated transportation; and as a member of the Ohio Legislature most of his life, his revisions of the statutes abolished imprisonment for debt and set up a fair system of taxation. No other individual of those pioneering days displayed such singular devotion to the welfare of the state and its people regardless of his own health and income.

BELOW
This picture of the lock house on the Ohio Canal at the foot of Seneca Street, Cleveland, was painted about 1860.

TOP RIGHT
Daily line of Ohio Canal packets.

BOTTOM RIGHT
Eurastus Ives, who came to Cleveland from Utica, New York, in 1810, spent many months working on the Ohio Canal, and to him was given the privilege of steering the first boat through the Eleven-mile Lock at Independence. Later he was steersman on a canal boat that employed James A. Garfield.

BELOW
State repair boats, which plied the Ohio Canal, were used to keep the locks in good condition, repair the tow path, and mend breaks in the canal. The two between Akron and Cleveland housed the repair men and their families from March to October. This boat is passing the intersection of Stone Road and the canal. In the background may be seen the fur trader's cabin, built in 1827 at the time of the opening of the canal.

DAILY LINE OF OHIO CANAL PACKETS

Between Cleveland & Portsmouth.

DISTANCE 309 MILES—THROUGH IN 80 HOURS.

A Packet of this Line leaves Cleveland every day at 4 o'clock P. M. and Portsmouth every day at 9 o'clock A. M.

T. INGRAHAM, *Office foot of Superior-street, Cleveland,*
OTIS & CURTIS, *General Stage Office,* do. } AGENTS.
G. J. LEET, - - - - *Portsmouth,*

NEIL, MOORE & CO.'S Line of Stages leaves Cleveland daily for Columbus, via Wooster and Hebron.
OTIS & CURTIS' Line of Stages leaves Cleveland daily for Pittsburgh, Buffalo, Detroit and Wellsville.

James G. Cowles

James G. Cowles

117

James G. Cowles

James G. Cowles

TOP LEFT
The scenic beauty along the canal encouraged the building of luxury canal packet passenger boats. A trip down the canal was a pleasant journey and a day of recreation.

BOTTOM LEFT
The Eleven-mile Lock between Rockside and Stone Roads was ready for use in 1827.

BELOW
Boats travelling between Highland and Alexander in Valley View, north of Willson's Mills, passed this beautiful tree at the right, now designated as a Moses Cleaveland Tree, indicating it was here in 1796.

OPPOSITE: TOP
This was Fourteen-mile Lock, north of Willson's Mills. The Cuyahoga River ran parallel with the canal on the other side of this house. There was only 10½ feet of ground for the tow path.

OPPOSITE: BOTTOM LEFT
Typical of industry along the Ohio Canal was the Palmer Organ Factory not far from Granger Road between the old covered bridge and the Mill Creek Aqueduct, Cuyahoga County. This photo of Mr. Palmer and his factory, reportedly taken in 1853, shows the site where the Baltimore and Ohio eventually laid their tracks.

OPPOSITE: BOTTOM RIGHT
This advertisement in the Cleveland Directory, 1837, indicates the importance of the canal to shipping merchants.

James G. Cowles

119

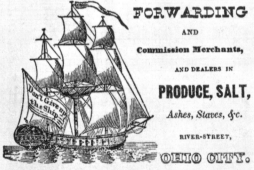

BARSTOW & CO.

FORWARDING

AND

Commission Merchants,

AND DEALERS IN

PRODUCE, SALT,

Ashes, Staves, &c.

RIVER-STREET,

OHIO CITY.

AGENTS FOR THE

Pilot, Traders, Erie & Ohio Lines

ON THE ERIE CANAL,

AND PROPRIETORS OF

WASHINGTON LINE, OHIO CANAL.

Liberal advances made on Property to be shipped or sold.

ABOVE

The Milan Canal Company was incorporated in 1827. Stock having a par value of $50 was issued to the amount of $35,000. In addition, $20,000 in bonds were sold. Because of dissension, work on the canal did not begin until 1833. Construction of a tow path from the mouth of the Huron River to Abbotsford was completed the next year and by 1836 enough money was raised to build the Canal Basin at Milan. The Milan Canal was officially opened on July 4, 1839.

BELOW

In the 1820's and 1830's Milan (Erie County) was a normal thriving Western Reserve settlement with its gristmill, sawmill, tannery, cabinetmaker, shoemaker, blacksmith, wagon works, and numerous stores. But with the completion of the Milan Canal in 1839 the town boomed. It became the busiest grain port in the world, rivaling, so they claimed, the Russian city of Odessa. Towns east, west, and south of Milan also prospered as they brought, besides millions of bushels of grain, their cattle, lumber, potash, barrel staves, and whiskey to be shipped to eastern markets and even to European countries. Warehouses, lining the canal banks, were filled to the brim with wheat, corn, and oats ready to be loaded on waiting boats. For ten long years endless lines of wagons deposited their treasures at Milan.

Without realizing the coming importance of the railroads, Milan made no attempt to encourage a line through the town. The canal seemed all sufficient. However, railroads were increasing all over the state as merchants chose the quicker method of transportation, and almost before Milan realized what was happening, the canal sank into decay and the town gradually settled back to the simple hamlet of previous decades. Even today it is difficult to visualize a bustling lake port of the 1840's in this typically New England village.

Sail and Steam

RIGHT

Levi Johnson (1786–1871) undoubtedly has more "firsts" added to his name than any early settler in the Reserve. Coming from Herkimer, New York, to Cleveland in 1809 when the settlement contained only log cabins, he built the first frame building, the first frame house, the first courthouse and jail, and even the first gallows (used only once to hang an Indian named O'Mic). In 1812 he was chosen the first county coroner and first deputy sheriff. A skilled carpenter and joiner, a conscientious workman, fair in all his dealings, his services were in constant demand. He was even called to Wakeman and Tinker's Creek to build their first sawmills. In 1824 he launched the first steamboat built in Cleveland, the 220-ton Enterprise with space for travelers as well as freight. This marked the beginning of Cleveland's importance in lake traffic. In 1830 he built the first brick lighthouse. His is the story of "from poverty to riches," for he came to the Reserve almost penniless, but before his life span ended he had accumulated a fortune.

Western Reserve Historical Society

LEFT

The Fairport Lighthouse, Lake County, was built by Jonathan Goldsmith in 1825.

BELOW

By 1830 Lake Erie commerce was booming and there was need for a lighthouse near the mouth of the Cuyahoga. Levi Johnson, master builder, was awarded the government contract of $8,000 to erect a brick tower on Water Street facing the lake. This sketch was made on the scene in 1856 by John Kilburn of Cincinnati.

Fairport Historical Society

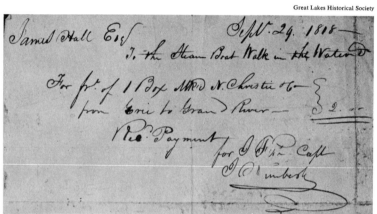

TOP LEFT

Walk-in-the-Water, the first steamboat on Lake Erie, was built at Black Rock near Buffalo in 1818. Dragged by oxen into deep water, she began her first trip, arriving in Cleveland to the salute of guns on August 25th. She had a speed of eight to ten miles per hour and a capacity of 100 passengers and 300 tons of freight. The fare from Black Rock to Cleveland was $10 including board. Passengers continuing on to Detroit paid an additional $5. The boat was wrecked near Buffalo in 1821, but the engine was saved and placed in the Superior, the second steamer on Lake Erie, in 1822.

MIDDLE LEFT

Bill of Lading, covering shipment on Walk-in-the-Water:
  James Hall, Esq.   September 29, 1818
    To the Steam Boat Walk in the Water, Dr.
    For frt of 1 Box mdse., N. Christie & Co.
    From Erie to Grand River $2.00
      Rec'd Payment
                    for J. Fish, Capt.
                    J. C. Stinbeck

BOTTOM LEFT

The Island Queen (U.S. #12092) was a side-wheel passenger boat built at Kelley's Island in 1854. It ran from Sandusky to the Lake Erie Islands, then to Toledo and Detroit.

BELOW

This view of Sandusky, Erie County, from the harbor is preserved on a platter of historical Blue Staffordshire. The side-wheeler, the Henry Clay, depicted in the center, was built in 1825. Early in the nineteenth century Staffordshire potters sent artists to this country to make sketches of our cities and landscapes. The Columbus and Detroit platters in this series have the same flower and scroll border. Although these platters have no potter's marks, the borders indicate that they were made by J. & R. Clews of Cobridge. The date of the Sandusky platter is about 1835. At this time the population of Sandusky was around 3,000.

TOP RIGHT
The brig Columbia was built in Sandusky in 1842. It carried the first cargo of iron ore into Lake Erie from Lake Superior in 1855. It was lost in Green Bay in 1859.

BOTTOM RIGHT
The Empire, built in Cleveland in 1844, was considered the largest steamboat in the country. This 1,200-ton side-wheeler attracted wide attention because of the unusual services offered on the speedy thirteen-hour trip from Cleveland to Buffalo. The $5 fare included entertainment and music by Leland's Band, cabins sumptuously furnished, and meals in a dining cabin on the upper deck.

BELOW
The Portsmouth (U.S. #19619), built at Buffalo in 1853, was called a "railroad line" boat because it was used as an extension of the Erie Railway, carrying passengers and packaged freight, at first from Dunkirk to Sandusky, later from Buffalo to Sandusky.

Great Lakes Historical Society

Great Lakes Historical Society

Gordon Wendt, Sandusky

In the 1853 *Gleason's Pictorial Drawing-Room Companion,* Sandusky was described as follows: "Sandusky, like most Western cities, has grown with that magical rapidity peculiar to this continent. It has 6,000 inhabitants, with numerous docks, public buildings and numberless craft constantly going and coming. The steamer in the foreground is a faithful portrait of one of Reed's line of steamers, plying from Buffalo to Toledo, touching at Erie, Cleveland, and Sandusky. These steamers are unsurpassed for speed and comfort."

A ferry was the logical answer for some transportation before the advent of bridges. The ferry at Black River (Lorain, Lorain County) carried passengers, cattle, and supplies across the river. A schooner had just been launched from the ways at the left. The large building at the right was the Reid House built in 1835 by Conrad Reid to replace the log tavern kept by his father, John S. Reid. In the early pioneering days John's three daughters —Elizabeth, Ann, and Sophia—took turns running the ferry.

Lorain County Historical Society

The 1853 *Gleason's Pictorial Drawing-Room Companion* described Cleveland in this manner: "In the early part of the year 1800, there was just one family residing in Cleveland; its present population is about 20,000. A small part of the city lies on the Cuyahoga River, where the land is but little elevated above the level of the lake, but it rises by a steep ascent to a level of some eighty feet above the lake, and on which gravelly plain this city is built. The location is one of the finest on Lake Erie—a view from it of the shipping and steamboats in the port, and leaving and entering the harbor, and the numerous vessels under sail on the lake, afford a prospect varied and beautiful. So extensive is the lake that it has all the grandeur of an ocean view. The harbor of Cleveland is one of the best on the lake, being spacious and safe and sufficiently easy of access. Cleveland was incorporated as a city in 1836 and owes its name to Moses Cleaveland, formerly of Canterbury, Ct. who directed the surveying party that first laid it out. Like all our Western cities, it hourly increases in wealth, and the number of its population, and bids fair to be, in time, a second Cincinnati."

This is a view of the lake shore about 1849 showing the completed John G. Stockley (or Stockly) Pier, extending 924 feet into the lake, with the Empire State and the Queen City docked along side. A few years earlier, Clevelanders had scoffed at Stockley's newest lakefront improvement, convinced it would have the same fate as the first pier in 1816, when a lake storm battered it beyond repair. No one had had courage or funds since then to make another attempt. But Stockley's pier withstood the storms, thus giving encouragement to others. By 1853 six piers had been built east of the river.

125

Bridges and Railroads

BELOW

This bridge, built prior to 1820, is the longest single span in Ashtabula County. It is 154 feet long and has both arch and truss construction. It crosses the Grand River at a bend in the Mechanicsville-Windsor Road, three miles southwest of Austinburg.

LEFT

This interior view of the Mechanicsville covered bridge shows the sturdy arch and truss construction.

126

RIGHT

The only remaining covered bridge in Summit County is located on Oak Hill Road in the valley of the Cuyahoga River. There has been some dispute about when it was built; several sources say about 1856. It is 115 feet long; some of the timbers are 7 by 10 inches and the roof boards are 18 inches wide.

BELOW

John S. Casement has been credited with building this stone bridge over the Grand River at Painesville and laying the tracks for the Cleveland, Painesville, and Ashtabula Railroad in the 1850's. He became a general during the Civil War and went on to greater honors in railroad building, among them laying the Union Pacific tracks which were joined by a gold spike at Promontory Point, Utah, to complete the first transcontinental railroad.

Summit County Historical Society

Mrs. Harold Furlong for Lake County Historical Society

TOP LEFT

This unusual railroad bridge spanned Elk Creek, the east branch of the Chagrin River in Willoughby in 1854. The two enterprising gentlemen in the beaver top hats were probably making big plans to convert the valley timber into finished lumber to be hauled by rail to Cleveland where a building boom was already in progress.

BOTTOM LEFT

The Columbus Street bridge, scene of the famous "bridge war," was built by James S. Clark in 1835. It was given to the City of Cleveland the following year. It was 200 feet long, 33 feet wide and 24 feet high. It had stone abutments on each bank. The draw in the center allowed a vessel of 49-foot beam to pass.

BELOW

As usual, industry was found near the falls and the railroad of a community. This sketch of the Old Vaughn Grist Mill in Berea was made in 1854.

OPPOSITE: TOP RIGHT

Here is the first steam locomotive in the Western Reserve, purchased by the Mad River and Lake Erie Railroad of Sandusky, which was chartered in 1832. The Sandusky was the first ever built by Rogers, Ketchum, and Grosvener of Paterson, New Jersey, a firm previously involved in the manufacture of cotton spinning machinery. Until

its final merger with the American Locomotive Company, this company and its legal successors built some 6,300 engines. On October 8, 1837, the Sandusky had its initial test in New Jersey prior to its shipment to the city for which it was named. It had to be conveyed via the Erie Canal and Lake Erie to Sandusky.

BOTTOM RIGHT
Map of Ohio Railroads. By 1855 railroads were the accepted mode of travel and the swiftest means of transportation. Ohio was supplied with a criss-cross network of railroads which connected many lines and intercepted the canals. Two northern terminals were Sandusky and Cleveland; Columbus, Cincinnati, and Dayton were busy southern terminals.

BELOW
The Sandusky, built in 1837, was a wood-burning engine with gigantic stacks to catch sparks and coupled drive wheels to make steep grades. The gauge of wheels was measured to fit the tracks of the Mad River and Lake Erie Railroad, 4 feet-10 inches wide. Each railroad had its own gauge.

Paul F. Laning, Sandusky

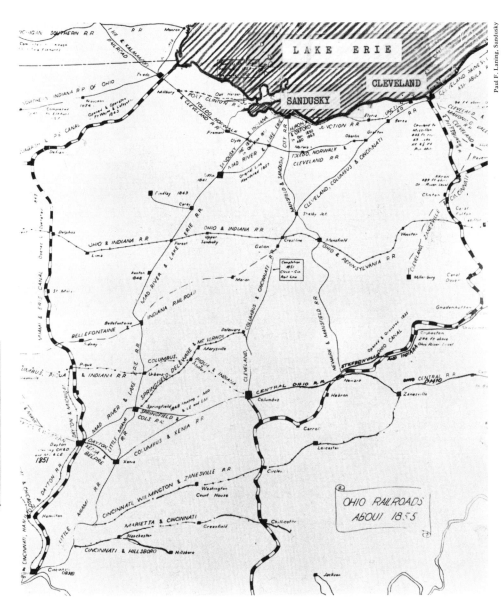

Paul F. Laning, Sandusky

129

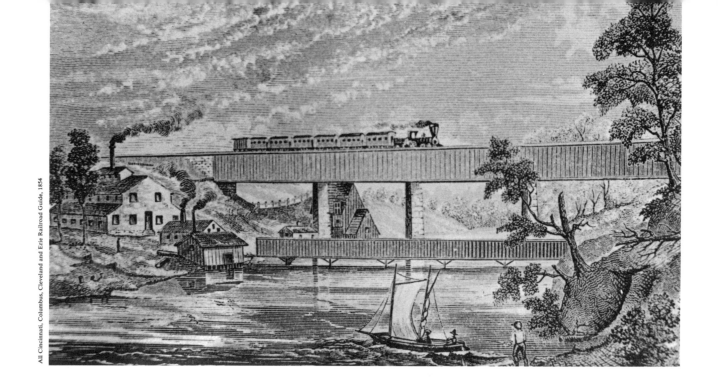

ABOVE

Industry and transportation have always been closely coupled. This is a good illustration showing both water and train transportation for the Geauga Furnace Company located on the west bank of the Erie Street hill in Painesville. The sketch was made in 1854.

BELOW

The railroads purchased right-of-way along the lakefront in Cleveland despite the protests of John G. Stockley, builder of the second pier, who tried to arouse the community to the need of preserving the shoreline for parks and a few docks. He lost his almost lone fight in 1851. By 1854 this was the scene at the foot of Bank and Water Streets, where the new railway station had been built close to the six piers.

Banking

TOP RIGHT

General Simon Perkins (1771–1844) was one of the very earliest settlers connected with the finances of the Westtern Reserve. As an agent for the Erie Land Company in 1798, he recorded some of the first land transactions on the above desk, which with paintings of his wife and home are on display at the Western Reserve Historical Society. For twenty-three years he conducted the affairs of the Western Reserve Bank at Warren, the first in the Reserve and one of the few banks which operated almost without interruption even through the worst panics. As a member of the Ohio Canal Fund Commissioners, he realized the importance of Akron as a strategic point on the canal. He purchased acreage in Akron and helped to lay out the town, thus building a future for his son Colonel Simon, who became Akron's leading citizen and a state senator, and for his grandson George, who became president of B. F. Goodrich and Akron Rubber.

MIDDLE RIGHT

The Western Reserve Bank at Warren was organized in 1812 in the midst of the second war with England, the first bank in the Western Reserve. Its chief asset was the men who organized it, and the chief security for the money it issued was the character of the men who stood behind it. For the first three years of its existence the bank operated in a frame structure, but in 1815 it moved into a new two-story brick as seen above. That year they loaned the State of Ohio $15,000 at 6% interest. The State agreed to exempt the bank from all taxes during the term of the loan. The first large loan of $50,000 went to the Ohio Canal commissioners of which bank president Simon Perkins was a member.

In 1844 it reorganized as a state bank, later it became a national bank and finally merged with the Citizens Savings and then the Warren Savings to become the Union Savings & Trust as it is known today. It has the enviable reputation of never having failed to redeem its paper in silver and gold coin even while other banks were failing.

BOTTOM RIGHT

The first Bank of Sandusky was organized in 1834. Ten years later this bank and the one in Norwalk were the only two authorized banks in the Reserve. Two years later it became a state bank under the new system of branches and continued as such until 1855. (No picture of this bank could be found.)

The Union Bank shown here with its imposing pillars was incorporated in 1851 and did business under that name till 1855. One wall of the bank was also the wall of the adjoining stone house, the first in Sandusky, built in 1821 by Eleutheros Cooke, the town's first lawyer.

131

TOP LEFT

Upper: The Western Reserve Bank at Warren was specially authorized to reorganize in 1845, and continued business almost without interruption.

Middle: The Forest City Bank issued this ten dollar bill in 1858.

Lower: This Bank of Sandusky ten dollar bill was issued in 1848.

MIDDLE LEFT

The Kirtland Safety Society, contrary to law at the time, issued this three dollar note #2059 on January 4, 1837. It was signed by Joseph Smith and Sidney Rigdon who inserted the word "anti" before Bank and added "ing" as if that would make it legal. They were both convicted of operating a bank outside the law.

BOTTOM LEFT

Upper: This bill for two dollars was issued by the Bank of Geauga, organized in 1829 and chartered as an independent state bank in 1845.

Middle: Bank of Norwalk bill for one dollar, issued in 1846.

Lower: The Merchants Branch Bank in Cleveland, one of five state banks formed in 1845, issued this ten dollar bill in 1848.

BELOW

The Bank of Geauga was built by Jonathan Goldsmith at the corner of Main Street and the park in Painesville in 1836 at a cost of $5,000. Moses Thompson of Perry made the brick for the building "down by the bayou at the south end of High Street in Fairport." Harvey Woodworth was head mason on the job.

TOP RIGHT

The name of Truman P. Handy (1807–1898) and banking became almost synonymous in the Cleveland area. Wherever a difficult situation occurred, especially during the Panic of 1837, his advice was sought. After some banking experience in Geneva and Buffalo, New York, he came to Cleveland to help resuscitate the Commercial

Bank of Lake Erie. Under his guidance it thrived until 1842 when the charter expired. He then started a bank of his own. In 1845 he organized the Commercial Branch Bank of Ohio of which he became cashier and manager. He also became president of the Merchants Branch Bank.

MIDDLE RIGHT

In the Western Reserve in the early nineteenth century, any silver was scarce. English, Spanish, and other silver coins were used along with United States coins. Here are some examples. Left to right, they are: 1840 United States dollar, 1800 Spanish dollar or piece of eight, 1821 United States ten-cent silver coin, 1834 United States five-cent silver coin, 1818 Crown with head of George III, worth five shillings.

BOTTOM RIGHT

The first bank in Cleveland and the second in the Reserve was the Commercial Bank of Lake Erie. Organized in 1816 with Alfred Kelley as president and Leonard Case as cashier, it was located on the northeast corner of Superior and Bank Street. It failed in 1820, was reorganized in 1832, functioned for ten more years, and went out of existence when its charter expired. For a time, the Merchants Branch Bank had its headquarters here. It later became the Merchants National Bank. This was also the first site of the Society for Savings Bank.

BELOW

One of the most dependable banks in the Reserve was the Bank of Norwalk, organized in 1831. When the State Bank of Ohio was authorized by law, five branches were established in the Reserve; Norwalk was one of them, receiving a charter in 1847. John Gardiner, who had served as cashier in the early bank, was named cashier and manager for the state bank, a position he held through its entire existence. Before 1860 the bank moved into new quarters in the St. Charles Hotel building (shown here). When the State Bank closed its doors, Gardiner was granted a charter for the Norwalk National Bank of which he became president.

133

A unique type of bank was organized in Cleveland in 1849: the Society for Savings, its object "to enable industrious persons to invest such part of their earnings as they can conveniently spare to advantage." It differed from most banks and savings and loan associations, in that it had no capital and was managed by trustees without salary in the interest of the depositors only. The first location was a basement room at 4 Bank Street, but by 1857 prosperity forced them to seek larger quarters in the Weddell House across the street. For 110 years it was known as a savings bank, but in 1958 it became Society National Bank.

Cuyahoga Falls Real Estate Association issued this five dollar note in 1838.

Ohio Land Company of Medina issued this three dollar note in 1838.

Ohio Railroad issued this two dollar note in 1840.

The Canal Bank of Cleveland issued this ten dollar note in 1852. It had been chartered as an independent state bank in 1845, but failed in 1854. Dr. H. C. Ackley, a trustee of the State Insane Asylum at Newburg, had deposited with the Canal Bank $9,000 of the institution's funds and some of his own. He made no issue over his own money, but demanded return of funds for the care of patients. When the bank refused, he swore out a writ of attachment and with the sheriff's assistance used a sledge hammer to break down the brickwork around the inner vault. To prevent further damage, bank officials gave them keys to the safe. They collected $400 in gold and $1,460 in bills—all the money there was.

134

Industry and Commerce

TOP RIGHT

These advertisements from *The Cleaveland Register* of September 1, 1818, illustrate the difficulty of obtaining cash. Evidently the boot and shoe-making business was not profitable for David Jones. Ads for the sale of salt and hats warranted prime space in the newspaper.

BOTTOM RIGHT

The village blacksmith, renowned in song and story, was a most important person in the early communities, when well-shod horses provided the best means of transportation.

BELOW

The itinerant cobbler was a welcome visitor in any settlement in the earliest days of the Reserve. Each family provided hides of animals which they had cured and tanned, and then eagerly supervised the making of necessary footgear.

135

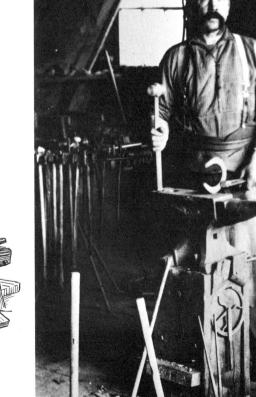

NOTICE.

The Subscriber having quit
The Boot & Shoemaking business,

In Cleaveland, requests immediate settlement, with all those, who have had dealings with him, previous to this date.
DAVID JONES.
Cleaveland, Aug. 6, 1818—3t

For Sale.

NEAR the Centre of Newburgh, a valuable Tan Yard, with Two Acres of Ground, in a high state of cultivation—a new dwelling house 22 by 32 feet square, one and an half stories high, with a room under ground. Lying within 30 rods of a good Grist mill, Saw mill, Fulling mill, Carding machine and Still house.
Also a Ten Acre Lot. For terms apply to the subscriber on the premises.
WM. L. PEETS.
Newburgh, Ang 11, 1818—3t

NOTICE.

ALL persons indebted to me, by book account or note, are requested to come and settle the same, and save cost.
Donald McIntosh.
Cleaveland, Aug. 18—3t

S. WALSWORTH.

Hat Manufacturer.
Keeps constantly on hand a general assortment of
Ladies, Gentlemen's and Boys HATS,
Of the first quality, all of which he will sell at the most reduced prices for cash, either wholesale or retail. Merchrnts who will favor him with their wholesale custom, may depend on having hats as low as they can be purchased in New York, and a liberal credit given.
All persons indebted, are requested to call and make, immediate payment.
☞ Three good workmen at the above business, would find constant employment and generous wages, by immediate application.
S. W.
Cleaveland, Aug. 18, 1818—tf

S. S. DUDLEY, & Co

HAVE THIS DAY PURCHASED.
160 Barrels Salt in addition to their old stock, which they offer to sell at $7 00 Cash. Those who wish to purchase their year's supply low would do well to make immediate application, as salt is on the rise.
Cleaveland, Aug. 11, 1818.—3t

Berea Historical Society

LEFT

In order to remove obstacles to settlement of new communities, the Connecticut Land Company encouraged the ownership of mills. William Wheeler Williams, who started the first gristmill and sawmill in the Reserve in 1799, received as his bounty a hundred-acre lot, the iron for a gristmill, and $150. Contemporary evidence has indicated that he did not build the mill himself but engaged Major Ezra Wyatt. For several years this was the only mill in Cuyahoga County and settlers made entire day trips to reach it. Only part of the original mill is shown in the center of this picture, the additions came much later. The mill stood near the present Miles and Broadway in Cleveland until the Pennsylvania Railroad tore it down in 1904 to relocate its tracks.

BELOW

Elyria's old Red Mill stood near the East Falls and the wooden Washington Avenue bridge. To the right are remnants of a factory.

136

RIGHT

In 1827 Colonel Luther Trumbull of New York purchased a sawmill on this site, Route 528 in Madison Township. He then added a woolen mill and in association with Homer Griswold operated both successfully for years.

BELOW LEFT

The first frame gristmill in Chagrin Falls was built at the south side of the falls in 1836 by George Fenkell. The wood siding was hauled by oxen from Shalersville. Drilling the pit for the water wheel out of solid rock was a long and arduous task. A dam was put across the river a few feet from the top of the falls and a race extended to the north bank of the river to furnish power for a nearby factory.

BELOW RIGHT

As early as 1803 a mill stood on this site in Youngstown, but it was not called Lanterman Mill until 1846 when German Lanterman built a house and a new mill in its place. At one time the water power not only ran the gristmill, but a sawmill, a furnace, and an ax factory. The mill is now a museum in beautiful Mill Creek Park.

137

LEFT

The entire family had a share in making a comfortable pioneer bedroom. Ladder-back chairs, simple bedsteads, and trundle beds with rope springs were made by the men. The womenfolk made cornhusk mattresses, rugs, patchwork quilts, and wove fine linen sheets. Often an itinerant weaver would set up his loom in a home to make needed coverlets. This lovely one with a bird and flower design was made by James Pearson of Chatham Township, Medina County, who proudly wove his name in two corners. His pay for several weeks' work might have been room and board, some staples, and very little money.

MIDDLE LEFT: Spinning wheel corner.

BOTTOM LEFT: Boston Rocker and candle stand.

BOTTOM MIDDLE: Ladder-back chair.

BELOW: Kitchen cupboard.

OPPOSITE: TOP

Early household needs were met by the crude skill of men and boys, who attempted to make articles necessary for everyday use. These were made by some of the first settlers in the Reserve. The bench came from the home of Dr. Jared P. Kirtland, the mortar and pestle from an 1812 tavern in Ravenna, and the bowl was made by James Nicholson, first permanent settler in Lakewood.

OPPOSITE BOTTOM: Bedroom scene.

138

*athaniel Chapman's mark a square crop
of the end of the right ... and a halfpenny the
underside of the same. Feb. 2. 1809.

...ph Harte mark a small crop off from
... right ear and a spade in the end of the
...re.   March 1st 1811.

...ham Blakeley's mark a small crop
... from the left ear and a spade in the end
... the same.   March 4th 1811.

... on Norton's mark a half crop the under
... of the left ear. April 1st 1811.
... by Moses H Smith

...than Spragues's mark a slanting crop
... from the under side of the left ear.
              June 20th 1811.*

Tallmadge Historical Society

Henry Howe, sketch by Steir

Dealer in Bolting Cloths and Mill Furnishing generally.

JOSEPH HAYWARD,
French Burr Mill Stone Manufacturer,
No. 46 Merwin-Street, Cleveland, Ohio.

Cleveland Directory, 1837

TOP LEFT

One duty of the township clerk was to record cattle marks. The clerk who recorded these in Tallmadge in 1809 and 1811 insisted that the right ear of an animal was the ear to the right of the person facing the beast, therefore these early cattle marks are all transposed. The register of cattle marks ends in 1850 for it was about this time that the state began to pass laws prohibiting animals to run at large.

MIDDLE LEFT

The early settlers waged continual battle against wild bears, wolves, foxes, weasels, and other predators of their livestock. Pigs, chickens, sheep, and even cattle were being ravaged at an alarming rate in Medina County until the people felt that some drastic action should be taken. They therefore sent a proclamation to nearby settlements announcing a concentrated hunt in the vicinity of Hinckley the day before Christmas, 1818, and invited them to join in an attempt to wipe out the wildlife preying on their stock. Approximately 500 men and boys gathered, and at a given signal closed in on a designated area slaughtering all the animals that crossed their paths. They reportedly killed three hundred deer, twenty-one bears, seventeen wolves, and countless smaller animals, many of them

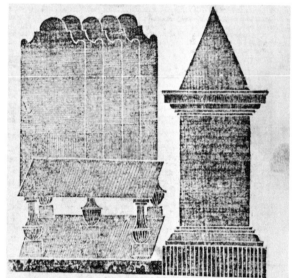

Cleaveland Register, September 1818

A. B. GARLICK.

STONE CUTTER, FROM NEW YORK.

INFORMS the public, that he carries on the stone cutting business in general, in the village of Cleaveland, where he intends to keep on hand an elegant assortment of Tomb Tables, Tomb Stones, and Monuments. of all sizes and descriptions, which can be had at short notice, elegantly carved, and lettered. Also, under-pinning, water-tables, window-caps, and stools for buildings.

All orders from the country, directed to Dr. D. Long, or the subscriber, will be punctually attended to.

☞ The above stone are procured from Dr. Long's quarry, it being far superior to any other discovered in this country.
Cleaveland, Aug. 18, 1818

quite harmless. The game was divided proportionately between the settlements participating. Stories about the hunt have been enhanced by retelling over the years, but it undoubtedly was one of the largest mass killings of wildlife in the Western Reserve.

OPPOSITE: BOTTOM LEFT
Advertisement of Burr Mill Stone Mfg.

OPPOSITE: BOTTOM RIGHT
Advertisement of a stone cutter

TOP RIGHT
One of the earliest industries in Peninsula was making grindstones. The large ones, called millstones, were used for grinding grain; the smaller ones for sharpening tools.

BOTTOM RIGHT
The early settlers of Amherst soon learned the value of the sandstone in the area and used it in building their homes. Not until later in the century was it in wide demand because of its superior quality. This is one of the early pits.

BELOW
By chance, John Baldwin discovered that stone found in the riverbed at Berea lent itself to sharpening a knife. Within a short time he developed a flourishing grindstone industry which brought him great wealth and made the name of Berea known throughout the world. He used his money to found Baldwin Institute (later Baldwin-Wallace College) and schools in other parts of the country and in faraway India.

Grace Goulder file

Grace Goulder file

141

LIVERY STABLE.

KIRK & WEEDEN,
Bank street, Cleveland,

Beg leave to inform the citizens of Cleveland and Ohio, and the public generally, that they continue to keep two horse Carriages, Gigs, Phætons, Barouches, Omnibusses, Buggies, and double and single Sleighs, for hire.

Horses bought and sold on reasonable terms, and Carriages for hire to go to any part of the United States.

☞ Horses kept by the night, week or month, n reasonable terms.

LEFT
Livery stables flourished at a time when horses furnished much of the transportation.

BELOW LEFT
Johnny Appleseed's trek throughout Ohio started many orchards, which in turn gave rise to prosperous cider mills. This one just east of Norwalk did a thriving business.

BELOW RIGHT
This cheese factory in Clarksfield Township, Huron County, provided cheese for many nearby country stores.

BOTTOM
The early sawmills were a boon to house and church building and the laying of plank roads. This one was located in Greenwich, Huron County.

TOP RIGHT

The raising of bees became quite a hobby in the early 1800's and a part of many farms was fenced off for an apiary. Honey and maple syrup vied with each other for a place on the farmer's table. Typical of most back yard apiaries was this one in Fitchville Township, Huron County.

MIDDLE RIGHT

Flax was easy to raise in the Western Reserve. In the very earliest days each housewife spun her own linen, but demand and more money encouraged the industry on a larger scale. This is a view in the yards of the New London Flax Mills.

BOTTOM RIGHT

Corn husking was a family industry. The corn provided food for the household and cattle; the husks were made into doormats and mattresses. This scene is on a farm in North Fairfield, Huron County.

BELOW

A silver medal was presented to Charles Messer for the power corn sheller which he exhibited at the Ohio State Fair held in Sandusky in 1858. He also manufactured threshing machines.

Picturesque Huron

Picturesque Huron

Picturesque Huron

143

ABOVE

The nucleus of a village was started by Alanson Pomeroy when he donated the land for a church adjacent to his country store and his homestead. This is one of the few homes in the area, built in 1848, that has remained untouched (even to its picket fence) by the progress rushing past its busy intersection in Strongsville. In the olden days, worshippers who lived too far away were invited to stay to dinner. The spare room was always available for itinerant preachers, teachers, or travelers. It was also a haven for runaway slaves, often carried to Cleveland as part of a load of hay, then put aboard a lake boat for Canada.

TOP LEFT

A blacksmith shop adjoins the residence of R. T. Page in Gates Mills, Cuyahoga County.

BOTTOM LEFT

Samuel Sears had only a few steps to walk from his home to his country store, where he sold flour, feed, dry goods, and groceries. The second floor was reserved for temperance meetings in the Brooklyn community.

BELOW

S. W. Knapp of Gates Mills operated a rake factory next to his residence.

ABOVE LEFT

Lucky was the family with a springhouse for they had free refrigeration. Built of stone over a fresh-water spring, it provided excellent storage for butter, cheese, eggs, milk, and meat. This one was located in Greenfield Township.

ABOVE RIGHT

This scene in Gates Mills shows the preparation of winter's ice for storage until needed in summer. Ponds and small lakes froze to their greatest depths during January and February. The ice was then cut in large blocks with horse-drawn and handsaws, packed in sawdust, and stored ready for use in tall "ice houses."

BELOW

These two advertisements from the 1837 Cleveland Directory indicate the beginning of a prosperous city. With the Ohio Canal and Lake Erie transportation booming it was possible to bring in many things that had been unavailable a year or two earlier. This marked the beginning of pictorial advertising in the Western Reserve.

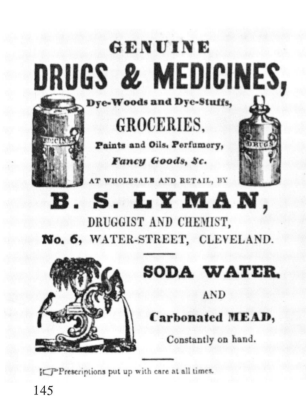

GENUINE
DRUGS & MEDICINES,
Dye-Woods and Dye-Stuffs,
GROCERIES,
Paints and Oils, Perfumery,
Fancy Goods, &c.
AT WHOLESALE AND RETAIL, BY
B. S. LYMAN,
DRUGGIST AND CHEMIST,
No. 6, WATER-STREET, CLEVELAND.

SODA WATER,
AND
Carbonated MEAD,
Constantly on hand.

☞ Prescriptions put up with care at all times.

145

PETER M. WEDDELL & CO.
AT the old stand, on the corner of Superior and Bank Streets, (No. 1, Washington Block) so long and so favorably known to the public, keep constantly on hand a very extensive assortment of
DRY GOODS,
consisting in part of Broad Cloths, Cassimeres, Sattinets, Cotton, Linnen and Worsted Drillings, Merino Cassimers, Summer Cloths, black and colored Silks, India Satins, worked Collars and Capes, dress Hk'fs and dress Shawls, Muslin Edgings, thread and bobinet Laces and Edgings, red, white and black Merino Shawls, imitation Cashmeres and raw silk Shawls, Gothic furniture Prints, very fine white and red Flannels, French, English and American Calicoes, Bed-ticking, linen & cotton Sheeting and Shirting, double and single Damask, Birdseye and Russia Diaper, Moleskins, Umbrellas, Parasols, &c. &c.

Also, a few pieces of very choice CARPETS & RUGS, together with a carefully selected assortment of
FAMILY GROCERIES.
The very best of Teas, Laguira and Old Java Coffee, Sugars, Rice, Raisins, Salæratus, Mrs. Miller's Tobacco, Honey Dew and Plug Tobacco 7 years old, Hard Soap, &c.

To those who may favor the establishment with a call, we would say, that they may rest assured of fair and honorable dealing. All goods not as good as recommended, will be taken back, or ample remuneration will be made; that the prices of their goods are as low as at any other store, and many articles lower than can be found at the stores generally; and finally, after tendering our thanks to our old friends, we would respectfully invite those making purchases in our city, to make us a call, not to buy, unless they think it for their interest, but to inform themselves respecting prices, qualities, &c. &c.

PETER M. WEDDELL,
DUDLEY BALDWIN,
PETER P. WEDDELL.

Cleveland, August, 1837.

Mrs. Donald C. Stem

Tallmadge Historical Society

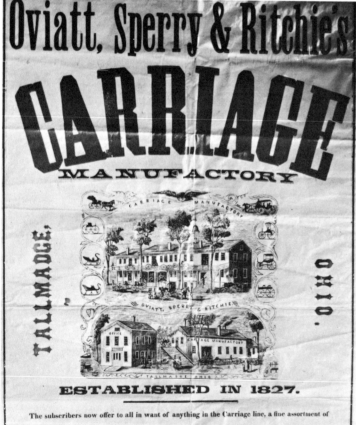

LEFT

One of Chagrin Falls' earliest industries was carriage making, as evidenced by the prominent place the Buckeye Carriage Works had in the village triangle. No attempt had been made to improve the roadway, but pedestrians rejoiced when new board sidewalks were introduced, and a plank strip made it possible to cross the street without sinking into the mud.

BELOW LEFT

For many years Tallmadge was famous for the quality of hand-made carriages and wagons. The first carriage works, which grew to have a large business in many states, began in 1827 in a log shop on the west side of the Park. Amos C. Avery, a native of Massachusetts, was the owner. In 1836 William C. Oviatt became his partner and the operation was moved to larger more modern buildings. Through the years there were various changes as one or more partners sold their interests. During its greatest prosperity it was known as the Oviatt, Sperry & Ritchie Carriage Manufactory.

BELOW

Bookseller's advertisement.

Cleveland Directory, 1837

YOUNGLOVE & WETMORE,

Wholesale and Retail

Booksellers, Stationers

AND BINDERS,

No. 40, Superior-street,

M. C. YOUNGLOVE.
EDW. F. WETMORE.

CLEVELAND.

Y. & W. keep constantly on hand an extensive collection of School, Classical, Theological, Law, Medical, and Miscellaneous Books; Stationery, of every description; Blank Books; Sheet Music; Cutlery; Fancy Articles, &c. &c. ☞ Books bound in the neatest manner, and at short notice.

They have also the Sabbath School and Tract Depository.

146

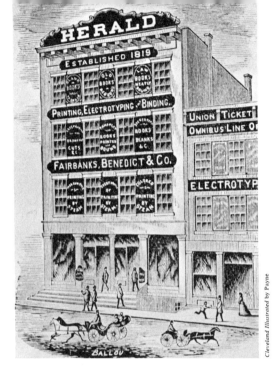

The Cleveland *Herald* was started as a weekly in 1819, but became a daily when it united with the *Daily Gazette* in 1837. The names of two of the 1850 proprietors, A. W. Fairbanks and George A. Benedict, have a prominent place on the front of the building.

MIDDLE RIGHT

The Chagrin Falls Paper Company's mill was built in 1841 by Noah Graves who learned his trade in Springfield, Massachusetts, before coming to the Reserve. This was one of the first paper mills in the state and it continued in operation until 1880. The Sack Factory was also operated by Noah Graves.

BOTTOM RIGHT

The year 1818 saw the birth of Lorain's first industry—shipbuilding. The first schooner launched in that year was the General Huntington. This is an early launching at Lorain, then known as Black River.

BELOW

Advertisement for books and job printing.

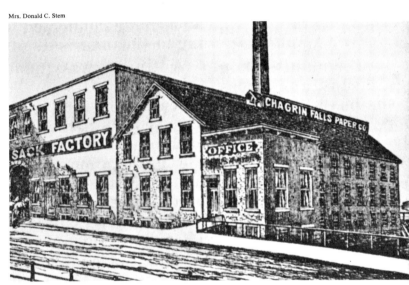

147

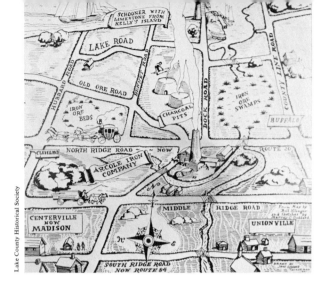

ABOVE

The above sketch showing ore beds, roads, charcoal kiln sites, shipbuilding, and loading docks, is an artist's attempt to illustrate the layout and activity of the Arcole Iron Company, originally known as the Erie Furnace Company when it was built in 1825 in Madison Township just south of North Ridge Road. Here were made heavy household stoves, hollow-ware, and potash kettles. The cast plates were shipped from the dock at the mouth of Cunningham Creek to Buffalo for assembly and sales.

BELOW

The Penfield Brick and Tile Plant was doing a prosperous business in Willoughby Center in 1853 when most of the labor was manual and done out-of-doors. An 1857 map of Lake and Geauga counties shows its location on the present Route 84 where the Pine Ridge Country Club stands. It was moved later to the south termination of Lost Nation Road in Willoughby.

OPPOSITE: TOP

The first explosive powder mill in the Western Reserve was established in Akron (1833) by the five Austin brothers, recently arrived from Vermont in search of a suitable place to manufacture black powder. They chose the section known as "Old Forge" where as early as 1816 a blast furnace, utilizing local bog ore and stone ore, had been operating. Local residents soon renamed the area "Powder Patch." The Ohio Canal nearby afforded quick transportation and was easily accessible to the coal mining industry, largest consumers of explosive powder. The Austin Company prospered with increased demands from coal companies, clay and stone quarries, sporting and rifle establishments. To facilitate deliveries additional plants were erected or purchased. After purchase of the Cleveland Powder Plant, operating since the 1850's at the Five-mile Lock in Newburg, the company moved its headquarters to Cleveland where it has been ever since.

The original Cleveland Powder Plant (opposite), constructed in the 1850's, was located in Newburg on 400 acres of land at the Five-mile Lock of the Ohio Canal. The area is now occupied by the Republic Steel and the Aluminum Company of America plants next to the Harvard-Denison bridge.

OPPOSITE: BOTTOM LEFT

This stone building at the Newburg plant of the Austin Powder Company is the type of mill used in 1833 for storage and preparation of nitrate of soda used in making black explosive powder.

OPPOSITE: BOTTOM RIGHT

Two wagons loaded with powder on the heel-path side of the canal are leaving the Austin Powder Company storage buildings.

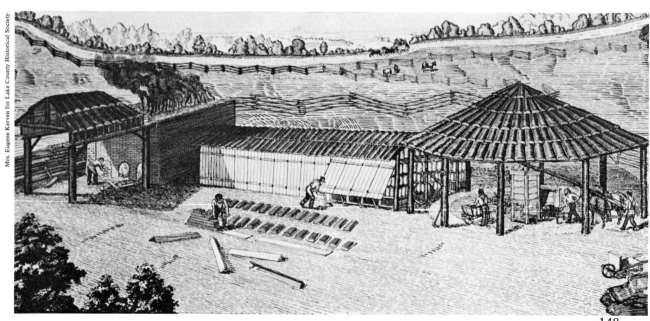

148

Austin Powder Company

Austin Powder Company

James G. Cowles

149

ABOVE

One of the first mills to bring luxury items to this area of the Reserve was the Pease Mill erected in 1850 on Girdled Road in Concord Township. Here Hiram Pease made fancy decorative wooden ware such as spice boxes, sugar pails, candle holders, and sewing aids.

BELOW

The Cleveland composite of 1851 shows the progress in transportation—covered wagon, Ohio Canal, first steamboat, Cleveland and Columbus stage line, Columbus and Cincinnati Railroad.

Acknowledgments

It is a difficult task to evaluate the help, encouragement, and inspiration I have received in gathering material for this book. A number of persons have secured original pictures and data which will add to our knowledge of the past, and often a casual suggestion has led me into a research project of historical importance.

Appreciation for sponsoring this project and encouraging me to complete it must be extended to Donald L. Harbaugh, President of the Early Settlers Association; to Herman L. Vail, President of The Western Reserve Historical Society; and to the joint advisory committee composed of Meredith B. Colket, Jr., Director of The Western Reserve Historical Society, Dr. Alexander Bunts, David K. Ford, and Robert C. Gaede. I am grateful that I have had the cheerful and dependable assistance of a fine photographer, V. Elroy Sanford, who was responsible for copying most of these pictures.

Dr. Merald Wrolstad of The Cleveland Museum of Art and my son Gerald W. Butler have been invaluable assistants in layout and criticism.

No historian of the Western Reserve could carry on research without the resources of the Cleveland Public Library and The Western Reserve Historical Society. Commendation must be given to Miss Donna Root, head of the History Division of the Cleveland Public Library and her able assistant Miss Janet Sanborn; and also to The Western Reserve Historical Society Librarian, Mrs. Alene Lowe White, and her helpers.

The following Trustees of the Early Settlers Association graciously listened to my progress reports and offered considerable advice: Judge Donald Lybarger, Clay Herrick, Jr., Mrs. H. J. Nord, Oliver Cromwell, Leo Weidenthal, Clarence Burge, and former trustees I. T. Frary and Benjamin P. Forbes, who dreamed about a book of this kind long ago.

Grateful acknowledgment is due Mrs. Grace Goulder Izant for placing at my disposal her collection of photographs, many of which are incorporated here, and to Edward S. Wells for the use of his historical library.

The following local historians and interested persons provided illustrations and information of particular value: Mrs. Alice Bliss, William K. Wilcox, Mrs. Donald C. Stem, Mrs. Dorothy M. McKelvey, J. Bruce Campbell, Bernard Vixseboxse, Robert Sidnell, Mrs. Ione K. Wiechel, Wallace B. White, Mrs. Robert Collacott, Mrs. James Cooper, George P. Metcalf, George K. Bishop, Ross Trump, F. E. Lawrence, Mrs. Robert Fletcher, Arthur H. Blower, and Norman Adams. I am also indebted to many others, too numerous to list here, who have responded graciously to my inquiries.

Bibliography

American Institute of Architects, *Guide to Cleveland Architecture.*

Anderson, Russell H., *The Rowfant Club* (Cleveland, 1955).

Andrica, Theodore, Series of articles on nationalities in *The Cleveland Press.*

Avery, Elroy McKendree, *A History of Cleveland and Its Environs* (3 vols., Chicago, 1918).

Badger, Rev. Joseph, *Memoirs* (1851).

Bates, James L., *Alfred Kelley, His Life and Work* (Columbus, 1888).

Beale, J. H., *Picturesque Sketches of American Progress* (New York, 1889).

Beers, J. H. & Co., *History of the Great Lakes* (1899).

Benton, Elbert Jay, *Cultural Story of an American City: Cleveland* (3 vols., Cleveland, 1943, 44, 46).

Bowen, Dana Thomas, *Lore of the Lakes* (Cleveland, 1940).

Brecksville Historical Association, *A Reminiscent History of Brecksville* (Berea, 1961).

Brooks, Katharine Gill, *Dunham Tavern* (Cleveland, 1938).

Butler, Margaret M., *The Lakewood Story* (New York, 1949).

Case, Eckstein, *The Ark* (Cleveland, 1902).

Cherry, P. P., *The Western Reserve and Early Ohio* (Akron, 1921).

Cherry, P. P., *Portage Path* (1911).

Clark, Edna Maria, *Ohio Art and Artists* (Richmond, 1932).

Cleave, E., *City of Cleveland and Cuyahoga County from Cleave's Biographical Cyclopedia of the State of Ohio* (1875).

Cleveland and Ohio City, *City Directory, 1837.*

Cincinnati, Columbus, Cleveland and Erie Railroad Guide (1854).

Coates, William R., *History of Cuyahoga County and the City of Cleveland* (3 vols., Chicago, 1924).

Conlin, Mary Lou, *The North Union Story* (pamphlet, Cleveland, 1961).

Dittrick, Howard, *Pioneer Medicine in the Western Reserve* (Cleveland, 1932).

Downes, Randolph C., *History of Lake Shore Ohio* (New York, 1952).

Early Settlers Association of the Western Reserve, *Annals 1880–1962.*

Fletcher, Robert, *History of Oberlin.*

Frary, I. T., *Early Homes of Ohio* (Richmond, 1936).

Frary, I. T., *Ohio in Homespun and Calico* (Richmond, 1942).

Gazette and Commercial, 1818 (Cleveland newspaper).

George, Milton C., *The Settlement of the Connecticut Reserve of Ohio, 1796–1850* (typescript, Ann Arbor, 1950).

Goodrich, S. G., *Recollections of a Lifetime* (2 vols., New York, 1856).

Grismer, Karl H., *Akron and Summit County* (1952).

Hatcher, Harlan, *The Western Reserve* (New York, 1949).

Hatcher, Harlan, *A Century of Iron and Men* (New York, 1950).

Havighurst, Walter, *Vein of Iron* (Cleveland, 1958).

Hawley, Dr. Zerah, *Journal of a Tour Through Connecticut, Massachusetts, New York, Pennsylvania, and Ohio* (New Haven, 1822).

Haydn, Hiram C., *Western Reserve University from Hudson to Cleveland* (Cleveland, 1905).

Hendrickson, Walter B., *The Arkites* (Cleveland, 1962).

Hodges, O. J., *Reminiscences* (Cleveland, 1902).

Horton, John J., *The Jonathan Hale Farm* (Cleveland, 1961).

Howe, Henry, *Historical Collections of Ohio* (numerous editions).

Hudson Garden Club, *Old Buildings in Hudson* (Pamphlet, 1962).

Huntington, C. C., *A History of Banking and Currency in Ohio Before the Civil War.*

Izant, Grace Goulder, *This is Ohio* (Cleveland, 1953).

Johnson, Crisfield, *History of Cuyahoga County* (Cleveland, 1879).

Kelley, Herman A., *A Genealogical History of the Kelley Family* (Cleveland, 1897).

Kennedy, James H., *A History of the City of Cleveland 1796–1896* (Cleveland, 1896).

Knittle, Rhea M., *Early Ohio Taverns* (Ashland, 1937).

Lane, Samuel A., *Fifty Years and Over of Akron and Summit County* (Akron, 1892).

Laning Printing Co., *Picturesque Huron* (1897).

Lindsey, David, *Ohio's Western Reserve: The Story of Its Place Names* (Cleveland, 1955).

Ludlow, Arthur, *Old Stone Church* (Cleveland, 1920).

Mahoning Valley Historical Society, *Historical Collections of the Mahoning Valley* (1876).

Mathews, Alfred, *Ohio and Her Western Reserve* (New York, 1902).

Melish, John, *Travels Through the United States 1806–09* (London, England, 1818).

Mills, William S., *The Western Reserve* (1900).

Orth, Samuel P., *History of Cleveland* (3 vols., Chicago, 1910).

Payne, William, *Cleveland Illustrated* (Cleveland, 1876).

Peeke, H. L., *The Centennial History of Erie County* (2 vols., Sandusky, 1925).

Perrin, William H., *History of Summit County* (Chicago, 1881).

Piercy, Caroline B., *The Valley of God's Pleasure* (New York, 1951).

The Plain Dealer, 1842 editions (Cleveland newspaper).

Post, Charles Asa, *Doans Corners* (Cleveland, 1930).

Rice, Harvey, *Pioneers of the Western Reserve* (Boston, 1883).

Rice, Harvey, *Sketches of Western Life* (Boston, 1887).

Robinson, W. Scott, (ed.), *History of the City of Cleveland* (Cleveland, 1887).

Rose, William Ganson, *Cleveland, The Making of a City* (Cleveland, 1950).

Roseboom, Eugene H., and Weisenburger, Frances P., *History of Ohio* (Columbus, 1953).

Shaw, Archer H., *The Plain Dealer: One Hundred Years in Cleveland* (New York, 1942).

Smart, Jermayne, *Folk Art of the Western Reserve* (typescript, Cleveland, 1939).

Tallmadge Historical Society, *A History of Tallmadge, Ohio* (1957).

Thoms, Herbert, *The Doctors Jared of Connecticut* (Hamden, Conn., 1958).

Tunis, Edwin, *Frontier Living* (Cleveland, 1961).

United States Dept. of the Interior, *Historic American Buildings Survey* (Washington, 1941).

Upton, Harriett Taylor, *History of the Western Reserve* (3 vols., Chicago, 1910).

Urann, C. A., *Centennial History of Cleveland* (Cleveland, 1896).

Waite, Frederick C., *Western Reserve University, The Hudson Era* (Cleveland, 1943).

Wallen, James, *Cleveland's Golden Story* (Cleveland, 1920).

White, Wallace, *One Hundred and Fifty Years: Milan Township and Village* (Milan, 1959).

Whittlesey, Charles, *Early History of Cleveland* (Cleveland, 1867).

Wickham, Gertrude Van R., *Memorial to the Pioneer Women of the Western Reserve* (4 vols., Cleveland, 1896–97).

Wilkinson, Helen H., *Gates Mills and a History of its Village Church* (Cleveland, 1955).

Williams, W. W., *History of the Firelands* (Cleveland, 1879).

Wing, George C., *Early Years on the Western Reserve, with extracts from Letters of Ephraim Brown and Family, 1805–45* (Cleveland, 1920).

Wittke, Carl, *We Who Built America* (1939).

World's History of Cleveland (1896).

Many communities in recent years have published booklets commemorating their early settlements:

Bedford Area 125th Anniversary, Inc., *Book of Bedford* (1962).

Greater Cuyahoga Falls Sesquicentennial Committee, *A History of Cuyahoga Falls* (1962).

City of Norwalk Sesquicentennial Book (1953).

Firelands Sesquicentennial Association, *Firelands Sesquicentennial Book* (1959).

Index

154

This book was composed in Linotype Times Roman and Typo Script by Davis & Warde, Inc., Pittsburgh; printed by lithography on 70-pound Mohawk Vellum by Great Lakes Lithography Company, Cleveland; and bound in Bancroft's Kennett by World Publishing Company, Cleveland. Design and typography by Merald E. Wrolstad